First World War
and Army of Occupation
War Diary
France, Belgium and Germany

29 DIVISION
86 Infantry Brigade,
Brigade Trench Mortar Battery
5 July 1917 - 31 August 1918

WO95/2302/8

The Naval & Military Press Ltd
www.nmarchive.com
Published in association with The National Archives

Published by

The Naval & Military Press Ltd

Unit 10 Ridgewood Industrial Park,

Uckfield, East Sussex,

TN22 5QE England

Tel: +44 (0) 1825 749494

www.naval-military-press.com

www.nmarchive.com

This diary has been reprinted in facsimile from the original. Any imperfections are inevitably reproduced and the quality may fall short of modern type and cartographic standards.

Contents

Document type	Place/Title	Date From	Date To
Heading	WO95/2302/8		
Heading	29th Division 86th Infy Bde Jly 1916 And 86th Trench Mortar Bty 1917 July To 1918 Aug		
Heading	War Diary For July 1917 By 86th Trench Mortar Battery Vol 29		
War Diary	Haandekot Bel & F L7 N.E.	05/07/1917	11/07/1917
War Diary	Proven Area No 2	12/07/1917	13/07/1917
War Diary	Zwanof Sector	13/07/1917	27/07/1917
War Diary	Proven Area No 3	26/07/1917	31/07/1917
War Diary	XIV Corps Front	31/07/1917	31/07/1917
Heading	War. Diary. For August 1917 From 86th Trench Mortar Battery Vol 29		
War Diary	Proven Area No 2	01/08/1917	03/08/1917
War Diary	Forest Area.	04/08/1917	11/08/1917
War Diary	Langemarck Boesinghe Sector.	12/08/1917	12/08/1917
War Diary	Forest Area	12/08/1917	27/08/1917
War Diary	Proven Area (P.3)	28/08/1917	31/08/1917
Miscellaneous	A Form. Messages And Signals.		
Miscellaneous	B.M. 22. To OC. 86 T.M. Bty	14/08/1917	14/08/1917
Miscellaneous	O.C., Royal Fusrs.	14/02/1917	14/02/1917
Miscellaneous	B.M. R 26	15/08/1917	15/08/1917
Operation(al) Order(s)	86th Brigade Order No 163	15/08/1917	15/08/1917
Miscellaneous	A Form. Messages And Signals.		
Operation(al) Order(s)	86th Infantry Brigade Order 168	25/08/1917	25/08/1917
Heading	War Diary For Sept 1917 Competed By O/C 86 T.M.B.		
War Diary	Pitt Camp	02/09/1917	13/09/1917
War Diary	Proven P3 Area	14/09/1917	15/09/1917
War Diary	Herzeele	16/09/1917	19/09/1917
War Diary	Proven. P.3 Area.	19/09/1917	19/09/1917
War Diary	Wellington Camp (Forward Area)	20/09/1917	20/09/1917
War Diary	Wellington Camp	21/09/1917	30/09/1917
Heading	86th T.M.B. War Diary For October 1917. 29		
War Diary	Wellington Camp.	01/10/1917	05/10/1917
War Diary	Harrow Camp	06/10/1917	08/10/1917
War Diary	White Mill Camp	08/10/1917	09/10/1917
War Diary	Proven P.5 Area	10/10/1917	15/10/1917
War Diary	Pretoria Camp P.5 Area	16/10/1917	16/10/1917
War Diary	Blairville Camp No 2	17/10/1917	31/10/1917
Miscellaneous	86th T.M. Battery Programme Of Work For Week Ending. 27/10/17	27/10/1917	27/10/1917
Miscellaneous	86th T.M. Battery Programme Of Work For Week Ending. 3/10/17	03/10/1917	03/10/1917
Heading	86th T.M. Battery War Diary For December		
War Diary	Masnieres	01/12/1917	01/12/1917
War Diary	Brown Line	02/12/1917	02/12/1917
War Diary	Rubicourt	03/12/1917	03/12/1917
War Diary	Havrincourt Wood	04/12/1917	04/12/1917
War Diary	Fins	05/12/1917	06/12/1917
War Diary	Houvin-Houvigneul	07/12/1917	16/12/1917
War Diary	Flers	17/12/1917	17/12/1917

War Diary	Wamin	18/12/1917	18/12/1917
War Diary	Verchocq	19/12/1917	31/12/1917
Miscellaneous	All Units.	01/12/1917	01/12/1917
Operation(al) Order(s)	86th Infantry Brigade Order No. 194	01/12/1917	01/12/1917
Miscellaneous	Warning Order	02/12/1917	02/12/1917
Miscellaneous	6 Units BC 26	02/12/1917	02/12/1917
Miscellaneous	A Form. Messages And Signals.		
Operation(al) Order(s)	86th Infantry Brigade Order No. 195	04/12/1917	04/12/1917
Operation(al) Order(s)	29th Division Administrative Order No. 22		
Heading	Attach to HQ 86 Infy Bde Dupl July to Dec 17		
Heading	War Diary D.A.G. Base		
Heading	War Diary For July 1917 86 TM Bty Dupl July To Dec 17 To Be Attached to HQ 86 Infy Bde.		
Miscellaneous	To D.A.G. 3rd Echelon Base	06/04/1918	06/04/1918
War Diary	Haandekot Bel & F 27 N.E.	05/07/1917	11/07/1917
War Diary	Proven Area No 2	12/07/1917	13/07/1917
War Diary	Zwanof Sector	13/07/1917	27/07/1917
War Diary	Proven Area No 3	26/07/1917	31/07/1917
War Diary	XIV Corps Group	31/07/1917	31/07/1917
Heading	Diary for July 1917 86 T.M.B.		
Heading	War Diary For August 1917		
War Diary	Proven Area No 2	01/08/1917	03/08/1917
War Diary	Forest Area.	04/08/1917	11/08/1917
Heading	August 1917 86th T.M.B.		
War Diary	Forest Area	11/08/1917	11/08/1917
War Diary	Langemarck-Boesinghe Sector.	12/08/1917	12/08/1917
War Diary	Forest Area	12/08/1917	27/08/1917
War Diary	Proven Area (P.3)	28/08/1917	31/08/1917
Heading	War Diary For September 1917		
War Diary	Proven P.3 Area	01/09/1917	01/09/1917
War Diary	Pitt Camp	02/09/1917	13/09/1917
War Diary	Proven P.3 Area	14/09/1917	15/09/1917
War Diary	Herzeele	16/09/1917	19/09/1917
War Diary	Proven. P.3 Area	19/09/1917	19/09/1917
War Diary	Wellington Camp (Forward Line)	20/09/1917	20/09/1917
War Diary	Wellington Camp	21/09/1917	30/09/1917
Heading	War Diary For October 1917		
War Diary	Wellington Camp	01/10/1917	05/10/1917
War Diary	Harrow Camp	06/10/1917	07/10/1917
War Diary	White Mill Camp	08/10/1917	09/10/1917
War Diary	Proven P.5 Area	10/10/1917	15/10/1917
War Diary	Pretoria Camp P.5 Area	16/10/1917	16/10/1917
War Diary	Blairville Camp No 2	17/10/1917	31/10/1917
Heading	Diary for October 1917		
Heading	War Diary For November 1917		
War Diary	Blaireville Camp No 2	01/11/1917	17/11/1917
War Diary	Haut-Allaine	18/11/1917	19/11/1917
War Diary	Equancourt	20/11/1917	20/11/1917
War Diary	Villiers Pluich	21/11/1917	21/11/1917
War Diary	Marcoing	22/11/1917	23/11/1917
War Diary	Masnieres	24/11/1917	30/11/1917
Heading	War Diary For November. 1917		
Heading	War Diary For December 1917		
War Diary	Masnieres	01/12/1917	01/12/1917
War Diary	Brown Line	02/12/1917	02/12/1917
War Diary	Rubicourt	03/12/1917	03/12/1917

War Diary	Haurincourt Wood	04/12/1917	04/12/1917
War Diary	Fins	05/12/1917	06/12/1917
War Diary	Houvin-Houvigneul	07/12/1917	16/12/1917
War Diary	Flers	17/12/1917	17/12/1917
War Diary	Wamin	18/12/1917	18/12/1917
War Diary	Verchocq	19/12/1917	31/12/1917
Heading	War Diary For December 1917		
Heading	86th T.M. Battery War Diary For January 1918		
War Diary	Verchocq	01/01/1918	03/01/1918
War Diary	Esquerdes	04/01/1918	16/01/1918
War Diary	Brandhoek	17/01/1918	17/01/1918
War Diary	Welsh Camp	18/01/1918	26/01/1918
War Diary	Brake Camp	27/01/1918	31/01/1918
War Diary	Brandhoek.	01/02/1918	03/02/1918
War Diary	Welsh Camp	04/02/1918	11/02/1918
War Diary	Poperinghe	12/02/1918	19/02/1918
War Diary	Eecke	20/02/1918	28/02/1918
Heading	War Diary For March 1918		
War Diary	Eecke	01/03/1918	07/03/1918
War Diary	Brake Camp	08/03/1918	12/03/1918
War Diary	Welsh Camp	13/03/1918	14/03/1918
War Diary	Battery. H.Q In The Line	15/03/1918	17/03/1918
War Diary	In The Line	17/03/1918	31/03/1918
Operation(al) Order(s)	86th Infantry Brigade Order No. 208		
Miscellaneous			
Operation(al) Order(s)	Addendum To 86th Infantry Brigade Order No. 209	14/03/1918	14/03/1918
Operation(al) Order(s)	86th Infantry Brigade Order No. 209	13/03/1918	13/03/1918
Operation(al) Order(s)	86th Infantry Brigade Order No. 210	16/03/1918	16/03/1918
Operation(al) Order(s)	86th Infantry Brigade Order No. 211	19/03/1918	19/03/1918
Operation(al) Order(s)	86th Infantry Brigade Order No. 212	23/03/1918	23/03/1918
Operation(al) Order(s)	86th Infantry Brigade Order No. 215	24/03/1918	24/03/1918
Heading	Secret		
Operation(al) Order(s)	86th Infantry Brigade Order No. 214		
Operation(al) Order(s)	86th Infantry Brigade Order No. 215	28/03/1918	28/03/1918
Operation(al) Order(s)	86th Infantry Brigade Order No. 216	29/03/1918	29/03/1918
Miscellaneous	Relief Table Issued With 86th Infantry Brigade Order No. 216 Dated 29th March 1918	29/03/1918	29/03/1918
Heading	86th Brigade. 28th Division. 86th Light Trench Mortar Battery April 1918		
War Diary	Brake Camp	01/04/1918	03/04/1918
War Diary	In The Line	04/04/1918	07/04/1918
War Diary	Brake Camp	08/04/1918	09/04/1918
War Diary	Neuf Berquin	10/04/1918	11/04/1918
War Diary	Pradelles	12/04/1918	12/04/1918
War Diary	St Sylvestre Cappel	13/04/1918	19/04/1918
War Diary	Hondeghem	20/04/1918	27/04/1918
War Diary	Nieppe Forest	28/04/1918	30/04/1918
Miscellaneous	2/R Fus.	09/04/1918	09/04/1918
Miscellaneous	A Form. Messages And Signals.		
Miscellaneous	Messages And Signals.		
Heading	War Diary For May 1918. HQ 86 Infy Bde Vol Trench Mortar		
War Diary		01/05/1918	31/05/1918
Miscellaneous	Raid to be carried out by 86th Infantry Brigade on night of 5th /6th May 1918	05/05/1918	05/05/1918
Miscellaneous	86th Inf. Brigade No. G. 92/22	05/05/1918	05/05/1918

Miscellaneous	86th Inf. Brigade No. G. 92/28	14/05/1918	14/05/1918
Miscellaneous	Amendment to 86th Inf. Brigade Order No. 223	18/05/1918	18/05/1918
Operation(al) Order(s)	86th Infantry Brigade Order No. 223	18/05/1918	18/05/1918
Miscellaneous	A Form. Messages And Signals.		
Operation(al) Order(s)	86th Infantry Brigade Order No. 222	15/05/1918	15/05/1918
Operation(al) Order(s)	86th Infantry Brigade Administrative Order No. 27. Issued With Brigade Order No. 224	18/05/1918	18/05/1918
War Diary		01/05/1918	30/06/1918
Heading	W R R Diary For June. 1918		
Heading	War Diary For July 1918 L T M B		
War Diary	Heuringhem	01/07/1918	21/07/1918
War Diary	Noordpeene	22/07/1918	31/07/1918
Heading	86th Trench Mortar Battery War Diary For August. 1918		
Heading	War Diary For August 1918		
War Diary	Noordpeene	01/08/1918	02/08/1918
War Diary	Borre	03/08/1918	31/08/1918

W095/2302/8

29TH DIVISION
86TH INFY BDE

~~LT. TRENCH MORTAR BTY~~
JLY 1916 AND.
86TH TRENCH MORTAR BTY

~~JLY - DEC 1917~~
1917 JULY to 1918 AUG

4

29

WAR DIARY

for

July 1917

by

8th Trench Mortar Battery

Army Form C. 2118.

Instructions regarding War Diaries and Intelligence Summaries are contained in F. S. Regs., Part II. and the Staff Manual respectively. Title Pages will be prepared in manuscript.

WAR DIARY
or
INTELLIGENCE SUMMARY

(Erase heading not required.)

Place	Date	Hour	Summary of Events and Information	Remarks and references to Appendices
HAANDEKOT Bd & F 27 N.E.	5/7/17	12.00	The battery marched to PROVEN AREA No 2 & was accomodated in tents & billets (F.9.a 5.9 1/20,000 27 N.E.	
	6/7/17		Strength reduced from 53 to 52 (1 Cpl admitted hospital. (V)	
	11/7/17		During the above period training was carried out daily, the weather fine & warm	
PROVEN AREA No 2	12/7/17	18.15	1 No 1 Section (1st Half) marched to CORRIDOR TR, ZWANOF SECTOR & relieved the 88th T. M. B.	
	13/7/17	14.00	No 1 Section (2nd Half) relieved 88th T.M.B in BAIRD TR, HUDDLESTONE TR, & NILE TR	
ZWANOF SECTOR		18.00	No 2 Section relieved remaining half of 88 T. M. B in CORRIDOR TR. Relief was carried out during day light & was completed by 19.00 (Map Ref Sheet 28 NW 2 1/10,000. C.13)	
	16/7/17	02.00	CEASERS NOSE bombarded*, great damage was done duckboards & other debris was seen flying in all directions *(Guns in HUDDLESTONE TR)	
	17/7/17	16.30	No 2 Section (CORRIDOR TR) relieved No 1 section in front system, relief carried out during daylight & completed by 17.00.	
	18/7/17		BOMBardment commenced, 1st Royal Fusiliers raided C.13 b. 8.9 (6 Prisoners) NEWFOUNDLAND Regt & 1st Essex Regt raided enemy lines at C 7 d 18 70, C 13 b 90 78	
	18/7/17	21.00	A heavy barage was put down on the enemy's trenches in response to S.O.S sent up by division on our right. Heavy enemy retaliation. Heavy casualties amongst regt holding line	
	19/7/17	01.45		
	19/7/17		bombardment increased, enemy retaliation slight, weather during day unsettled	

2449 Wt. W14957/M90 750,000 1/16 J.B.C. & A. Forms/C.2118/12.

Instructions regarding War Diaries and Intelligence Summaries are contained in F. S. Regs., Part II. and the Staff Manual respectively. Title Pages will be prepared in manuscript.

WAR DIARY
or
INTELLIGENCE SUMMARY
(Erase heading not required.)

Army Form C. 2118.

Place	Date	Hour	Summary of Events and Information	Remarks and references to Appendices
ZWANOF SECTOR	20/7/17	14.00	No 1 Section relieved by 38th DN & proceed to H CAMP	
	20/7/17	07.00	R.W.B raided enemys trenches at C. 7. a 60. 75. no prisoners. Slight enemy retaliation, 1 Gun Pit in HODDLESTONE TR partially destroyed 1 gun put out of action	attached orders
	21/7/17	18.00	Remainder of battery relieved by 38th DIV. Relief was completed by ~~1900~~ 16.00. ~~No 1 section~~	
		09.00	No 2 Section moved to ~~Proven~~ CORPS STAGING AREA ~~Camp~~	
			During this tour the weather was good, there were no casualties, at times enemy shelling was very heavy, several emplacements were partially destroyed & amount of work entailed considerable	
			From 21/7/17 to 23/7/17 Parades & training were carried out as usual.	
	24/7/17		The battery moved to PROVEN AREA No 3 & relieved the 88 T.M.B. One N.C.O & 6 men were temporarily attached to each battalion for the forthcoming operations, it was decided to alot each battalion 1 gun 6 mules & 1 GS wagon mules & wagons were supplied by the D.A.C. These guns will be controlled entirely by battalion commanders (One officer will probably be attached to each two battalions	
	25/7/17	08.30	Field day (Officers only attended) remainder of battery trained as usual	Ordr Attchd
	26/7/17		Training as usual	
	27/7/17	08.30	Field day (Officers only attended)	

2449 Wt. W14957/M90 750,000 1/16 J.B.C. & A. Forms/C.2118/12.

Army Form C. 2118.

WAR DIARY
or
INTELLIGENCE SUMMARY
(Erase heading not required.)

Instructions regarding War Diaries and Intelligence Summaries are contained in F. S. Regs., Part II. and the Staff Manual respectively. Title Pages will be prepared in manuscript.

Place	Date	Hour	Summary of Events and Information	Remarks and references to Appendices
PROVEN AREA No 3	26-7/17 to 30/7/17		Battery training as usual	
	31/7/17	00.15	The battery relieves the 87 T.M.B. in PROVEN AREA No 2. Weather wet & misty. All kit was reduced to a minimum — surplus sent to DUMP under Brigade arrangements. Strength increased from 48 to 64. Reserve personnel attached for duty. Brigade under 3 hours notice to move.	
		05.00	Advance commences.	
XIV Corps Front		10.50	Situation — 1 Guards Brigade believed to be from Railway U27 b 4.6 along western bank to U21 d.4.2 over Steenbeek opposite ROISSEAU FM. Line definitely reported along green line. Line in touch with FRENCH on green line at U20 c 5.7. Prisoners 11 off 237 OR unwounded. War material captured not reported.	Map Ref LANGEMARK 1/10000
		11.30	Hostile counter attack made on 38 DIV. at AU BON GITE U18 central completely smashed by Artillery, rifle & MG fire. Some prisoners taken from assaulting troops	

anh

4

29

Vol

WAR · DIARY

for

AUGUST 1917

from

86th Trench Mortar Battery

Instructions regarding War Diaries and Intelligence Summaries are contained in F. S. Regs., Part II. and the Staff Manual respectively. Title Pages will be prepared in manuscript.

WAR DIARY
or
~~INTELLIGENCE SUMMARY~~
(Erase heading not required.)

Army Form C. 2118.

Place	Date	Hour	Summary of Events and Information	Remarks and references to Appendices
PROVEN Area No 2	1/8/17		Heavy rain for 24 hours. Strength reduced 1 NCO & 1 OR returned to battalion — 67	
	2/8/17	08·30	3 hours notice cancelled. Total prisoners captured by 5th Army 120 off 5780 OR. by 14th Corps 772 OR. – wounded 2 off 244 OR one 10·5 cm How, 11 M.G., 27 T.M. & 2 L.T.M. Continued rain	
	3/8/17	15·30	Relieved 89th T.M.B in FOREST Area Camp A.4.d.9.3 (Ref 28.N.W BELGIUM 1/20,000). Bivouacs, tent – hut. Very muddy conditions & continued rain.	
FOREST AREA.	4/8/17		Continued rain	
	5/8/17		Weather conditions considerably improved – no rain. Slight enemy shelling of this area with long range guns. One man leave – one L/Cpl evacuated — Strength 66. Bombs were dropped in this area during the night	
	6/8/17	14·45	Bombs dropped by hostile aeroplanes. Weather still good	
	7/8/17		Weather still good	
		21·00	Heavy gun fire was heard, the barrage lasted until about 22·15	
	8/8/17	19·00	Weather showery	
	9/8/17	19·00	Camp moved to A.5.c.5.2 Weather good	
	10/8/17		Weather good. Enemy shelled vicinity of Rear Brigade Headquarters Camp A.4.d.9.3. about 22. with long range guns.	
	11/8/17	11	Orders received 11am to take 4 guns to support 16th MIDDLESEX in their	

2449 Wt. W14957/M90 750,000 1/16 J.B.C. & A. Forms/C.2118/12.

Instructions regarding War Diaries and Intelligence Summaries are contained in F. S. Regs., Part II. and the Staff Manual respectively. Title Pages will be prepared in manuscript.

WAR DIARY
or
~~INTELLIGENCE SUMMARY~~
(Erase heading not required.)

Army Form C. 2118.

Place	Date	Hour	Summary of Events and Information	Remarks and references to Appendices
FOREST AREA	11/8/17	11.00	Attack on PASSERELLE FARM U.21.c.62.95 (Ref. BIXSCHOOTE 20.SW4 1/10000). CAPT. J Blair White went up to reconnoitre returning 15.30.	
		18.00	Battery proceeded up the line. Capt J Blair White. Lieut McLaynes, 2/Lt A.W.G. Kellingly. Heavy thunderstorm 21.30.	
LANGEMARCK – BOESINGHE Sector	12/8/17	00.15.	On reaching CAPTAINS FARM. U.26.b.20.65 (Ref. LANGEMARCK 1/10000) the Battery was caught in a heavy hostile artillery barrage, suffering heavy casualties. (KILLED 3 O.R. DIED OF WOUNDS 2. WOUNDED 1.O. (Lieut McLaynes) 3 O.R.) Battery obliged to withdraw.	
FOREST AREA		5.00	Battery returned to camp. Roads bad. Ground from Advanced Bde HQ very muddy and cut up making progress slow. Weather showery.	
	13/8/17		Weather unsettled.	
	14/8/17	3.15	Enemy shelling this area with long range guns (1 O.R. KILLED). Received orders to hand over 1 Stokes Gun & team to each Batt. Received Brigade orders that 29th Division in conjunction with troops on Right & Left would attack the [illegible]; time to be notified later. Weather showery.	Attached orders. Attached orders
	15/8/17	2.00	Received orders that one Officer to accompany each of the Stokes Guns attached to 2nd Royal Inniskilling Fus. & 1st R.D.F.	Attached orders
		12.30	Capt J Blair White went with gun team attached to 1st R.D.F.	
		16.00	2nd Lt A.W.G. Kellingly went to join gun team attached to 2nd R.D.F. Received Brigade Order 163 reference operations 88th Brigade.	
		17.00	Received B.M.R. 26	Attached orders. Attached orders
	16/8/17	4.45.	Zero. 29th Division attacked.	

Army Form C. 2118.

WAR DIARY
or
INTELLIGENCE SUMMARY
(Erase heading not required.)

Instructions regarding War Diaries and Intelligence Summaries are contained in F. S. Regs., Part II. and the Staff Manual respectively. Title Pages will be prepared in manuscript.

Place	Date	Hour	Summary of Events and Information	Remarks and references to Appendices
FOREST AREA	16/8/17	12.15	Received news that the final objective has been captured in its entire length. Weather good.	Attached wire
	Night 16/17/8/17		86th Brigade & 1 Batt 87th Brigade take over new line from 87th & 88th Brigades	Attached orders
	17		Weather good	
	18	19.15 21.00	Capt J Blair White wounded. Hostile aircraft active over back areas. Bombs were dropped. Weather good.	
	Night 19/8/17		Lewis Gun of Middlesex Regt came out of the line. 2 men of Lewis Gun team manning gun out of action. Weather sleep good.	
	20	3.00	1 Officer (2/Lt R.C. Killingley) 2. O.R. wounded. Heavy shelling on front system. Weather good	
	Night 20/21/8/17		H^Q R.D.F. and 2 R.F. relieved.	
	21/8/17		Weather good	
	22/8/17	21.00 to 21.30	Hostile aircraft active. Bombs were dropped on FOREST AREA Weather good.	
	23/8/17		Gun teams attached to Batt^n rejoin the Battery.	
	24/8/17		Weather good.	
	25/8/17	10 am	1. Officer (2/Lt B Light 2 R F) and 9 O.R. taken on strength to replace casualties. 3 O.R. (attached returned to units being incompetent) Weather good.	

2449 Wt. W14957/M90 750,000 1/16 J.B.C. & A. Forms/C.2118/12.

Instructions regarding War Diaries and Intelligence Summaries are contained in F. S. Regs., Part II. and the Staff Manual respectively. Title Pages will be prepared in manuscript.

WAR DIARY
or
INTELLIGENCE SUMMARY
(Erase heading not required.)

Army Form C. 2118.

Place	Date	Hour	Summary of Events and Information	Remarks and references to Appendices
FOREST AREA	26/8/17		Weather good.	
	27/8/17		Weather unsettled	
PROVEN AREA (P3)	28/8/17		29th Division relieved by the GUARDS Division in the LEFT SECTOR.	
		11.00	86th Brigade moved to PROVEN. P3 AREA. Battery accommodated in PITT CAMP. (W.30.d.2.8) ref. map. (Sheet 19.S.E).	Attached orders
			Heavy rain	
	29/8/17		Work on Camp. Weather bad.	
	30/8/17		Received Bde orders re forming training and Bde Sport. No 21423 Pte Healey J. awarded Military Medal.	
			Weather improved.	
	31/8/17		Weather better.	
	~~1/9/17~~			

2449 Wt. W14957/M90 750,000 1/16 J.B.C. & A. Forms/C.2118/12.

"A" Form.
MESSAGES AND SIGNALS.

Army Form C.2121
(in pads of 100.)
No. of Message

Prefix Code m.	Words	Charge	This message is on a/c of:	Recd. at m.
Office of Origin and Service Instructions.	Sent At m. To By		Service. (Signature of "Franking Officer.")	Date From By

TO T.M.Battery. Royal Fus. Lancs.Fus. Middx. Regt. R.Dublin Fus.)for)inf.

Sender's Number	Day of Month.	In reply to Number.	AAA
* G 1	14th		

Please to arrange to hand over 1 Stokes Mortar and Team to each Battalion by 6-0 p.m. to-day.

F.H. Mum
Captain,
BdeMajor.

From
Place 86th Infantry Brigade.
Time

The above may be forwarded as now corrected. (Z)

Censor. Signature of Addressor or person authorised to telegraph in his name.

* This line should be erased if not required.

(7105) Wt W12093/M1217 50,000 pads. 1/17. D. D. & L. (E764.) Forms C/2121/11.

B.M. 22

(2) SECRET

To
O.C. 86 T.M. Bty.
Royal Fusiliers (for information)
Royal Dublin Fusiliers (")

Please detail an officer to go with each of the 11 Stokes Guns attached to the Royal Fusiliers and Royal Dublin Fusiliers.

14.8.17

T.F. Dearden Capt.
BM 86 Bde.

(3)

SECRET.

O.C., Royal Fusrs.
Lancashire Fusrs.
Middlesex Regiment.
Royal Dublin Fusiliers.
M.G.Company.
T.M.Bt tery.

A Sick Collecting Post has been established at Rear Brigade Headquarters (29./ A.5.c.1.2.) with a Medical Officer in charge.

Cases for evacuation or detention from Units in the FOREST AREA should be sent to this Station.

Capt.,
Staff Captain,
86th Infantry Brigade.

14/8/17.

SECRET. (4) BMR 26.

To. Royal Fusiliers
Lancashire Fusiliers
Royal Dublin Fusiliers.
Middlesex Regt
86 M.G. Coy
86 T.M. Bty

Zero hour for Z day (Aug. 16th) will be 4 45 am.

Acknowledge

F.F. Dearden Capt.
B M 86 Bde

15 8 17

(5)

S E C R E T.

Copy No 10

86th BRIGADE ORDER NO 168.

Reference Maps.
BIXSCHOOTE 1/10,000 and
ST.JULIEN, 1/10,000.

15th August, 1917.

1. On receipt of orders, the 86th Infantry Brigade and one Battalion (1st R.Inniskilling Fusiliers) 87th Infantry Brigade, will take over the RED Line from the assaulting troops on the night of Zero/Zero + 1 day, and will be distributed as follows:-

3 Battalions Front and Support Line.
1 Battalion GREEN Line (Brigade Support), and
1 Battalion BLUE Line (Brigade Reserve).

2. For purposes of Relief the line to be taken over will be allotted into areas as below, and any Battalion must be prepared to occupy any such area:-

AREA A. From Left Boundary of Division (inclusive) to U.16.c.1.6. (inclusive to Battalion occupying B. area as below).

AREA B. From U.16.c.1.6. (inclusive) to U.16.d.35.15. (inclusive).

AREA C. From U.16.d.35.15. (exclusive) to Railway at U.23.a.4.9. (inclusive of Strong Point on Railway).

AREA D. GREEN Line S.E. of point of junction with UNICORN Trench at U.15.d.8.2.

AREA E. The BLUE Line.

All Battalions will be distributed in depth, but Commanding Officers must satisfy themselves that their front line is sufficiently strongly held to repel any enemy counter attack. The consolidation and wiring of the position must be completed as soon as possible.

3. Battalions will be allotted to areas according to circumstances. and Headquarters of Battalions will keep in touch with 86th Brigade Headquarters at BOESINGHE CHATEAU, and notify their location after getting into position East of CANAL.

4. Battalions will take the following stores with them before going up to relieve:-

100 extra shovels (exclusive of shovels carried by 25/
100 screw piquets.
20 coils Barbed Wire.
40 tins of Water.

These Stores to be drawn from existing Dumps East of CANAL (Water tins can be drawn from ABRI WOOD).

"A" Form.
MESSAGES AND SIGNALS.

161

Army Form C.2121
(in pads of 100.)
No. of Message

Prefix Code m. | Words | Charge
Office of Origin and Service Instructions.
Sent
At m.
To
By

This message is on a/c of:
Service.
(Signature of "Franking Officer.")

Recd. at m.
Date
From
By

TO ~~Frosh~~ ~~Frog~~ ~~Frugal~~ ~~Friend~~ ~~Fraud~~ ~~Freight~~

Sender's Number	Day of Month	In reply to Number	AAA
* ~~S06/780~~	16		

Final objective has been captured in its entire length.

From ~~Fruit~~
Place
Time

The above may be forwarded as now corrected.
(Z) [signature] Captain.
Censor. Signature of Addressor or person authorised to telegraph in his name.

* This line should be erased if not required.

(7107) Wt. W12093/M1217 50,000 pads. 1/17. D. D. & L. (E764) Forms C/2121/11.

(7)

SECRET. Copy No. 10......

86th INFANTRY BRIGADE ORDER 168.

....

Reference Maps 1/20,000. AUGUST 25th 1917.
19.S.E. 27.N.E.
20.S.W. 28.N.W.

1.(a) The 29th Division will be relieved by the Guards Division in the LEFT SECTOR XIVth Corps commencing Aug.26th.

(b) The 86th Infantry Brigade will be replaced by the 1st Guards Brigade in the ELVERDINGHE AREA (B.9.c. and d.).

2. The relief will be carried out in accordance with Table "A" attached. The daily locations will be as shown in Table "B" attached.

3. During process of relief , Battalions and other units will be under tactical command of Brigadiers in whose area they may be.

4. Battalions will send on advance parties of 1 officer and 6 N.C.Os. to take over their respective camps. These parties to move early on the morning of the day their Battalions are due to take over the camps.

5. The Divisional Machine Gun Officer will arrange for the moves of the 86th M.G.Company in accordance with Table "A" attached.

6. Each Battalion will detail one officer to report to the Brigade Major at ZOMMERBLOOM CABARET one hour before their train is due to leave ELVERDINGHE.
Battalions to be at the Station twenty minutes before their train is due to leave.

7. Transport to move by road under orders to be issued by the Staff Captain.

8. Brigade Headquarters will close at ZOMMERBLOOM CABARET and reopen at W.30.d.6.7.., on the 28th instant at an hour to be notified later.

9 ACKNOWLEDGE

J.F. Dearden Captain,
Issued at 4.30 p.m. Brigade Major, 86th Inf.Brigade.

Copies to :-

1.3	Staff	11	Signals 86th Brigade.
4	Diary	12	No.2.Coy.Div.Train.
5	Royal Fusrs.	13	29th Division G.
6	Lancs.Fusrs.	14	do. Q.
7	Middx.Regt.	15	87th Brigade.
8.	Roy.Dublin Fus.	16	88th Brigade.
9	86/M.G.Coy.	17	1st Guards Brigade.
10	86/T.M.Bty.	18	3rd Guards Brigade.

19. Area Commandant PROVEN.

29

WAR DIARY

for

SEPT^R 1917

Compiled by O/C 86 T.M.B.

WAR DIARY
or
~~INTELLIGENCE SUMMARY.~~
(Erase heading not required.)

Army Form C. 2118.

Instructions regarding War Diaries and Intelligence Summaries are contained in F. S. Regs., Part II, and the Staff Manual respectively. Title pages will be prepared in manuscript.

86th Trench Mortar Battery

Place	Date	Hour	Summary of Events and Information	Remarks and references to Appendices
PROVEN. P.3	1/9/17		Weather good.	
AREA. PITT CAMP	2/9/17		Weather good	
	3/9/17		1. Officer (2nd Lt N. SAGAR 1st L.F.) taken on strength of ~~Battery~~. Weather still good	
	4/9/17	11am	Brigade inspected by Divisional Commander. Presentation of honours awarded for gallantry in the recent operations. No 21423 Pte J Healey (1st L.F. atta 86th TMB) Military Medal. Weather very fine	Atts orders.
	5/9/17		Weather good. 1 N.C.O Gas course.	
	6/9/17		Weather good.	
	7/9/17		Battery went for motor bus trip to coast. 2nd Lt N Sagar went on Trench Mortar course 5th Army School. Weather good.	
	8/9/17		Weather good. Hostile aeroplanes active at night over Back areas.	
	9/9/17		Weather still good. 1 O.R. struck off strength being evacuated to hospital.	
	10/9/17		Weather holds good hostile aeroplanes active at night. 2/Lt [illegible] R.F.A. (W. Mx) Regt. [illegible] appointed to 86th TMB with rank of A/Capt.	
	11/9/17		Weather good. 86th Brigade Sports in the afternoon.	
	12/9/17		Weather good.	
	13/9/17		1 O.R. taken on strength. 3 O.R. admitted to C.R.S.	

D. D. & L., London, E.C.
(A7863) Wt W809/M1672 350,000 4/17 Sch 52a Forms/C/2118/14

Instructions regarding War Diaries and Intelligence Summaries are contained in F. S. Regs., Part II. and the Staff Manual respectively. Title pages will be prepared in manuscript.

WAR DIARY
or
~~INTELLIGENCE SUMMARY.~~
(Erase heading not required.)

Army Form C. 2118.

86th Trench Mortar Battery

Place	Date	Hour	Summary of Events and Information	Remarks and references to Appendices
PROVEN P3 AREA	14/9/17		1 O.R. discharged from C.R.S. Weather good.	
	15/9/17		Weather good.	
HERZEELE	16/9/17		Battery moved to HERZEELE O.10.c 00.60 (Ref map BELGIUM FRANCE 27 N.E. 1/20000) in accordance with 86th Bde Order 170.	Atts Orders
	17/9/17		Training at HERZEELE.	
	18/9/17		1 Gun team reported to each Battn to co-operate in Training	
	19/9/17	9am	Brigade attack in accordance with 86th Bde Order No 172. 1 Gun team with each Battn. 2 guns in Brigade Reserve.	Atts Orders
		15.00	Battery moved back to PROVEN. P.3 AREA in accordance with 86th	Atts Orders
PROVEN. P.3 AREA.		17.00	Bde Order No 174, arriving at PITT CAMP 17.00.	
			From the 28/8/17 to 19/9/17 Brigade sports were organised in which the Battery took an active part	
WELLINGTON CAMP (Forward Area)	20/9/17	17.00	Battery relieved 3rd Guards T.M.B. in accordance with 86th Bde Order No 173 and 86th Bde Administrative Order No. 9. Battery accomodated in WELLINGTON CAMP 28.B.d.1.8 (Ref map BELGIUM 28 N.W.). Movement by train	Atts Orders
	20/9/17		Hostile aircraft active between 20.00 and 23.00. Weather good.	

Instructions regarding War Diaries and Intelligence Summaries are contained in F. S. Regs., Part II. and the Staff Manual respectively. Title pages will be prepared in manuscript.

WAR DIARY
or
~~INTELLIGENCE~~ SUMMARY.
(Erase heading not required.)

Army Form C. 2118.

86th Trench Mortar Battery

Place	Date	Hour	Summary of Events and Information	Remarks and references to Appendices
WELLINGTON CAMP	21/9/17		Battery engaged on work on camp. Weather good.	
	22/9/17		During the night vicinity of camp occasionally shelled with H.V. shells. Work on the camp. Hostile aircraft active during the day. 1 Officer (2/Lt Wingfield C.F. 1st RDF) + 1 O.R. taken on strength. Weather good.	
	23/9/17		Work on TRACK. 11 in accordance with Bde Orders G/81/19. Part allotted to Battery. from B.9.c.0.2 to stream at B.8.d.7.2 (ref map. BELGIUM.28.N.W) Hostile aircraft active over this area 20.00. to 23.00. Weather good	Att. order
	24/9/17		Work on TRACK. 11. Weather good.	
	25/9/17		Work on TRACK 11. Hostile aircraft active in the evening over this area and vicinity. Weather good	
	26/9/17		Work on TRACK 11. Two O.R. taken on strength. Weather good	
	27/9/17		Work on TRACK 11. E.A again active over this area. Bombs were dropped in the vicinity of ELVERDINGHE. Weather good	
	28/9/17	9.30	Working Party for TRACK 11.	
		17.15.	Two gun teams under 2/Lt B. LIGHT left camp to report to C.O 1st RDF.	

D. D. & L., London, E.C.
(A7883) Wt W869/M1672 350,000 4/17 Sch 52a Forms/C/2118/14

Instructions regarding War Diaries and Intelligence Summaries are contained in F. S. Regs., Part II, and the Staff Manual respectively. Title pages will be prepared in manuscript.

WAR DIARY
or
~~INTELLIGENCE~~ SUMMARY.
(Erase heading not required.)

Army Form C. 2118.

86th Trench Mortar Battery

Place	Date	Hour	Summary of Events and Information	Remarks and references to Appendices
WELLINGTON CAMP	28/9/17		at Battn HQ. at U.23. c. 08. 10 (Ref map. BROEMBEEK 1/10000). Guns in position at U.23. A. 60.98 and U.23. B. 58.30 (Ref map BROEMBEEK 1/10000)	
	29/9/17		Work on TRACK 11. Enemy Aeroplanes active over back areas during the evening weather good. Two gun teams under 2/Lt SAGAR went into the line & took up position at U.23. a. 60 91 (Ref map. BROEMBEEK 1/10000).	
	30/9/17.		Weather good.	

D. D. & L., London, E.C.
(A7883) Wt W809/M1672 350,000 4/17 Sch 52a Forms/C/2118/14

29

86TH
TRENCH MORTAR
BATTERY.
No.
Date

86th T. M. B.

WAR DIARY
for
October 1917

4

Instructions regarding War Diaries and Intelligence Summaries are contained in F. S. Regs., Part II. and the Staff Manual respectively. Title pages will be prepared in manuscript.

WAR DIARY
or
~~INTELLIGENCE~~ SUMMARY.
(Erase heading not required.)

Army Form C. 2118.

Place	Date	Hour	Summary of Events and Information	Remarks and references to Appendices
WELLINGTON CAMP.	1.10.17	2000	Two Gun teams under 2/Lt. Wingfield relieved 2/Lt Light and two gun teams in the line at U.23.a.60.90. (ref map M.1. 1/10000 attd). Weather good	
	2		Battery in the line. Forward H.Q. at U.23.c.15.75 (ref map. BROEMBEEK 1/10000)	
	3.		Guns in line ranging on targets in accordance with Barrage scheme laid down by 86th Bde. Two gun teams under 2/Lt. Light reported to	All orders
			O.C. Right Company. 1st R.D.F. behind EAGLE TR (U.23.b.60.25 ref map	All orders
	4.	2400	BROEMBEEK 1/10000) at midnight. Weather good.	
	4.		ZERO DAY. The two guns under 2/Lt LIGHT advanced behind Coast-wave by the 1st R.D.F. Remaining guns fired in accordance with 86th T.M.B. Barrage. 3 O.R. killed 1 Officer (2/Lt LIGHT) 3 O.R. wounded.	
	5.		On night of 5/6th 86th Bde relieved by the 4th Division.	
HARROW CAMP	6	11.45am	Battery relieved in WELLINGTON CAMP by 1st Guards Bde T.M.B. Battery accommodated in HARROW CAMP. Weather very bad.	All orders.
	7.	1600	2/Lt SAGAR and two gun teams went into the line with the 1st L.F. Position taken up at U.18.c.90.60 (ref map BROEMBEEK 1/10000)	
	8.	1600	Battery moved to WHITE MILL CAMP (B.15.a.02.70. 28 NW 1/20000)	

D. D. & L., London, E.C.
(A7883) Wt W809/M1672 350,000 4/17 Sch 52a Forms/C/2118/14

Army Form C. 2118.

Instructions regarding War Diaries and Intelligence Summaries are contained in F. S. Regs., Part II, and the Staff Manual respectively. Title pages will be prepared in manuscript.

WAR DIARY
or
INTELLIGENCE SUMMARY.
(*Erase heading not required.*)

Place	Date	Hour	Summary of Events and Information	Remarks and references to Appendices
WHITE MILL CAMP	8.10.17	1600.	Two gun teams under 2/Lt Wingfield went into the line at U.18. d. 90.60. Forward Headquarters were at U23. c. 05. 10. (ref map BROEMBEEK 10000) Weather bad.	All orders.
	9.10.17		ZERO DAY. Attack renewed by 29th Division in conjunction with troops on right & left. Two gun teams under 2/Lt SAGAR advanced behind rear wave of 1st L.F. Took up position at OLGA HOUSES U.18. b. 70.25 (ref map BROEMBEEK 10000). Casualties. 1 O.R. killed. 3 O.R. wounded. Battery relieved on the night of 9/10th.	All orders.
PROVEN P.5 AREA	10.	7am.	86th Bde having relieved accommodated in P.5 AREA. Battery accommodated in PRETORIA camp.	All orders.
	11		Weather unsettled.	
	12.		Weather unsettled.	
	13.		Battery inspected by G.O.C. Brigade. Weather still unsettled. Received warning order re move.	
	14.		Weather good.	
	15.		Received 86th Bde Order 183 re move. weather good.	

D. D. & L., London, E.C. (A7883) Wt W809/M1672 350,000 4/17 Sch. 52a Forms/C/2118/14

Instructions regarding War Diaries and Intelligence Summaries are contained in F. S. Regs., Part II, and the Staff Manual respectively. Title pages will be prepared in manuscript.

WAR DIARY
or
~~INTELLIGENCE SUMMARY.~~
(*Erase heading not required.*)

Army Form C. 2118.

Place	Date	Hour	Summary of Events and Information	Remarks and references to Appendices
PRETORIA CAMP ~~A5 AREA~~	16.10.17	1.25	Battery in accordance with 80th Bde Order 183 entrained at HOUPOUTRE 6.17.d (ref map 27 NE 1/20000). Detrained at BEAUMETZ. Marched	Attd Order
BLAIRVILLE	17.10.17	2.30	to Mn. camp BLAIRVILLE.	
CAMP No 2.	18.10.17		Court of Enquiry held to enquire into the alleged absence and deficiencies of kit of No. 3311 Pte Robinson S. 1st Z.A. Weather very good.	
	19.10.17		Improving camp. 1 Officer (2/Lt WINGFIELD) and 9 O.R. left Battery to rejoin 1st R.D.F.	
	20.10.17		1 Officer (2/Lt MARTIN) and 11 O.R. from 1st R.G.L.I. 1 Officer (2/Lt WATTS) and 4 O.R. from 2nd R.F. 6 O.R. from 16th Middlesex Regt taken on strength of Battery. 3 O.R. to Rest camp. Weather good.	
	21.10.17.		Weather fine.	
	22.10.17.		Training in accordance with attached programme. 1 O.R. leave to England. Capt S.R.D. Hinde four days rest at [illegible] CONVALESCENT CAMP.	Attd programme
	23.10.17.		Training. Weather bad.	

D. D. & L., London, E.C.
(A7883) Wt W809/M1672 350,000 4/17 Sch 52a Forms/C/2118/14

Instructions regarding War Diaries and Intelligence Summaries are contained in F. S. Regs., Part II, and the Staff Manual respectively. Title pages will be prepared in manuscript.

WAR DIARY

or

~~INTELLIGENCE SUMMARY.~~

(Erase heading not required.)

Army Form C. 2118.

Place	Date	Hour	Summary of Events and Information	Remarks and references to Appendices
BLAIRVILLE	24.10.17		Training. Weather bad.	
Area No. 2.	25.10.17		Weather very bad.	
	26.10.17	10.00	Brigade Ceremonial parade. Weather improved.	
	27.10.17	10.00	Brigade Ceremonial parade. Weather improved.	
	28.10.17		1 Officer (2/Lt HARTIN) & 7 O.R. admitted to hospital. Weather good	
	29.10.17		Training. Weather good. Two O.R. on Brigade Pigeon Flying course	
	30.10.17		Training. Practice for Brigade Ceremonial Parade.	
	31.10.17		Training. Capt. J.R.I. Hinde awarded the Military Cross.	

D. D. & L., London, E.C.
(A7883) Wt W809/M1672 350,000 4/17 Sch 52a Forms/C/2118/14.

86TH T.M. BATTERY

Programme of work for week ending 27/10/17.

DATE.	9 - 9 30	9.30 - 10.30	10-45 - 11.45	11.45 - 12.45	12.45 - 1
22nd Monday	P. T.	Arms Drill Squad Drill	Gun	Drill	Gun Inspection
23rd Tuesday	P. T.	Bayonet Fighting & Musketry.	Lecture on Fuzes	Digging Emp	lacements
24th Wednesday	P. T.	Arms Drill Box Respirator D.	— Firing	—	—
25th Thursday	P. T.	Bayonet Fighting Squad Drill	Musketry	on Range.	—
26th Friday	P. T.	Gun Drill	Digging Emplacements	Gun Drill	Lecture on Clinometer
27th Saturday	P. T.	Gun Drill	— Firing	—	—

86TH T.M. BATTERY

Programme of work for week ending 3/10/17.

DATE.	9 – 9.30	9.30 – 10-30	10.45 – 11.45	11.45 – 12.45	12.45 – 1
29th Monday	P. T.	Digging	Emplacements	—	—
30th Tuesday	P. T.	Lecture on Clinometer	Arms Drill	Box Respirator Drill	Gun Inspection
31st Wednesday	P. T.	— F	I R I N G	—	—
1st Thursday	P. T.	Squad Drill Bayonet Fighting	Musketry	on	Range.
2nd Friday	P. T	Gun	Drill	Musketry on Range	
3rd Saturday	P. T.	Gun Drill	— F I	R I N G.	—

86th T.M. BATTERY

WAR DIARY

for

DECEMBER

Army Form C. 2118.

Instructions regarding War Diaries and Intelligence Summaries are contained in F. S. Regs., Part II, and the Staff Manual respectively. Title pages will be prepared in manuscript.

WAR DIARY
or
~~INTELLIGENCE SUMMARY.~~
(Erase heading not required.)

Place	Date	Hour	Summary of Events and Information	Remarks and references to Appendices
MASNIERES	1/12/17		We had 3 guns at the Dump in LES RUEVERTES and fired about 30 rounds per gun. Enemy was driven out after severe fighting	
		16.30	Enemy again in LES RUEVERTES	
		19.00	First orders received re evacuation from 86th Brigade. We had 2 guns at the Dump in LES RUEVERTES, these were blown up by enemy shell fire. Our remaining gun was blown up by a bomb before evacuation. All spare men did stretcher bearing to expedite the evacuation of the wounded.	orders att. (1) (2)
		20.00	Final orders to evacuate	
		21.30	Battery withdrawn to BROWN LINE. This was done without any casualties. Our Casualties during the operations were 2 O.R. killed 2 Officers and 10 O.R. wounded and 2 O.R. missing	
BROWN LINE	2/12/17	11.00	Orders received from 86th Brigade to withdraw from BROWN LINE to TRESCAULT after dusk.	orders att (3) (4)
		16.45	Marched in rear of 16th MX. Regt. and reached TRESCAULT at 19.00 hours Here we found the men belonging to the Battery who had been stretcher bearing the previous evening.	

D. D. & L., London, E.C.
(A7883) Wt W8c9/M 672 350,000 4/17 Sch 52a Forms/C/2118/14

Army Form C. 2118.

WAR DIARY
or
~~INTELLIGENCE SUMMARY.~~
(Erase heading not required.)

Instructions regarding War Diaries and Intelligence Summaries are contained in F. S. Regs., Part II. and the Staff Manual respectively. Title pages will be prepared in manuscript.

Place	Date	Hour	Summary of Events and Information	Remarks and references to Appendices
			There being no accomodation at TRESCAULT orders [redacted] were received to march to RUBICOURT which we reached about 22.30 hours. Here we found 3 OR stragglers from the Battery. Heavy Enemy shelling in this village. 1 N.C.O. in advance	
RUBICOURT	3/12/17	11.30	Orders received to move to the neighbourhood of EQUNCOURT. Marched to HAVRINCOURT WOOD where we were accomodated in 4 Tents	orders att. (5)
HAVRINCOURT WOOD	4/12/17	9.30	Received orders to move to FINS	
		11.30	Marched to FINS which was reached at about 12.00 hours. Here we were accomodated in 4 Tents	
FINS	5/12/17	8.00	Received orders to move to ETRICOURT to entrain for PETIT-HOUVIN	orders att. (6)
		11.00	Marched to ETRICOURT which was reached at 12.00 hours. Entrained at 14.30 but did not leave until 16.30 on account of Enemy shelling the line.	
	4/12/17	5.30	Detrained at PETIT HOUVIN and marched to HOUVIN-HOUVIGNEUL which was reached at 9.30	

D. D. & L., London, E.C.
(A7883) Wt W809/M1672 350,000 4/17 Sch 52a Forms/C/2118/14

Army Form C. 2118.

Instructions regarding War Diaries and Intelligence Summaries are contained in F. S. Regs., Part II, and the Staff Manual respectively. Title pages will be prepared in manuscript.

WAR DIARY
or
INTELLIGENCE SUMMARY
(Erase heading not required.)

Place	Date	Hour	Summary of Events and Information	Remarks and references to Appendices
HOUVIN-	7, 8			
HOUVIG-NEUL	9, 10 &c		Resting in accordance with G.O.C's wishes. 1 O.R. on Course of Instruction Gas. Weather fair	
	11/12/17	11.30	Brigadier General's Parade. Battery Paraded with 1st R.G.L.I. Lieut G.S. Lawson was taken on strength and took over command of the Battery	
	12/12/17		2/Lieut A.E.H. SMITH taken on strength of Battery. Lieut MARTIN and 2/Lieut SAGAR returned to their respective units and were struck of strength of the Battery. Training	
	13/12/17–14/12/17		Training. Re-organisation of Detachments	
	15/12/17		13 O.R. taken on strength of Battery in accordance with 86th Brigade Instructions.	
	16/12/17	12.15	Marched to FLERS which was reached at 16.45. Heavy snow in afternoon	
FLERS	17/12/17	9.30	Marched to WAMIN which was reached at 16.30. Weather very bad in morning much snow & very heavy going. No one fell out.	
WAMIN	18/12/17	9.30	Marched to VERCHOCQ arriving at 17.00. Roads very bad, very stiff marching. No one fell out	

Instructions regarding War Diaries and Intelligence Summaries are contained in F. S. Regs., Part II. and the Staff Manual respectively. Title pages will be prepared in manuscript.

WAR DIARY
or
~~INTELLIGENCE SUMMARY.~~
(Erase heading not required.)

Army Form C. 2118.

Place	Date	Hour	Summary of Events and Information	Remarks and references to Appendices
VERCHOCQ	19/12/17		Resting accomodated in Billets	
	20,21			
	22	Dec	Training. Weather sever, frost & snow	
	23/12/17		1.O.R. taken on strength 1.O.R. to Hospital 1O.R. from Course of Instruction	(Gas)
	24/12/17		Training	
	25/12/17		Xmas Day	
	26,27			
	28,29	Dec	Training 1.O.R. from Hospital	
	30		1.O.R from Hospital 1.O.R to Hospital. Warning Orders received from Brigade re move	
	31/12/17		Training	

J. S. Lawson Lieut

D. D. & L., London, E.C.
(A7823) Wt W8o9/M1672 350,000 4/17 Sch 52a Forms/C/2118/14

(1)

All Units.

In the event of a retjrement from MASNIERES and LES RUES VERTES being ordered the following instructions will be carried out. The B.G.C. intends to hold the following line. The line now held by 88th Inf. Bde. as far as L.30.c.7½.7. thence along the ditch through L.30.a. G.25.b. to the Lock at L.24.c.7.4. thence the Reserve Line in 87th Brigade Sector from the ~~xxxxxx~~ Lock at L.24.c.7.4. to CHATEAU TALMA inclusive. The 86th Brigade will withdraw on both sides of the Canal, troops South of the Canal halting on the line of the Ditch through L.30.a. and those North of the Canal passing through the 87th Brigade and crossing the Canal by all available bridges west of the Lock in L.24.c.7.4. and will assemble in a positionw hich will be notified later. 87th Brigade will cover the retiremen t throwing back the right flank of the Inniskilling Fusiliess to the Canal in G.20.c. The South Wales Borderers will conform to the movement of the 86th Brigade and will withdraw to ~~xx~~ the line of the Ditch through L.30.a. assisting troops of the 86th Brigade to hold this line.

As soon as the 86th Bde. has crossed the Canal ~~x~~the Border Regiment & Inniskilling Fusiliers will retire simultaneously each Regiment covering its own retirement. The Border Regt. with one coy. of Inniskilling Fus. attachdd will hold the Reserve Line from the Lock in L.24.c.7.4. to CHATEAU TALMA inclusive. They will leave at least one a~~n~~ half companies in the defences of CHATEAU TALMA. The Inniskilling Fus. will cross the Canal by all available ~~xxx~~ bridges and will assemble in a position which will be notified.

[signature]

Brigadier General,
Commanding 86th Inf. Bde.

1/12/17.

(2)

86TH INFANTRY BRIGADE ORDER NO. 194.

Reference Map GOUZEAUCOURT.

1. The 86th Inf. Brigade will withdraw from MASNIERES to the Brown Line at L.34.Central tonight.

2. The withdrawal will commence at the following times:-

Troops in Rue VERTE (except those at Barrier)	11 pm
Clear by	11.30 p.m.
Royal Fusiliers	11.30 p.m.
Clear by	11.40 pm
Middlesex Regiment	11.40 pm.
Clear by	12.15 am.
Garrison of Barrier	12 midnight.
Bridgeheads at Lock in 27.a.	12.15 a.m.
Lancashire Fusiliers	12.15 am.
Clear By	12.45 am.
Bridgehead Defencers	12.45 a.m.

3. Bridgehead defences will be held as already detailed.

4. Route will be through CHATEAU Grounds - Light Railway - Cross CANAL at Lock Bridge at G.24.c - East side of MARCOING Copse - MARCOING - MARCOING VILLERS PLOUICH Road - L.34.Central.

An Officer of the Brigade Staff will be at the lock at G.24.c. and guides will be there.

5. Two guides per Battalion and one guide per smaller Units will report to Brigade Headquarters at once. They will meet Units on the VILLERS PLOUICH Road and conduct them to rendezvous.

6. Units will pass through a defensive line formed by the 87th Inf. Brigade on the approximate lines Stream through G.30 - Lock G.24.c. - Ammunition Pits in G.19.a.

7. The 1/Lancashire Fus. will warn the 1/8.Inniskilling Fusiliers when they have evacuated their position,

8. Battalions will withdraw by Platoons.

9. It must be impressed on all ranks that a withdrawal is a most difficult operation and must be conducted with the utmost secrecy. There will be no talking or smoking during the operation.

10. As Units clear the CHATEAU Grounds they will report to the Brigade Major or at Brigade Headquarters that their withdrawal is complete.

11. ACKNOWLEDGE.

[signature]

Captain,
Brigade Major,
86/Infantry Brigade.

1/12/17.

(3)

Warning Order BC 25

1. The 86th Inf. Bde will move from their present area this evening to the vicinity of the Wagon lines.
2. Arrangements are at present being made and detailed instructions will be issued as soon as possible
3. Units will render in strength Return by 3 pm to day. This should include personnel of Machine Gun Coy and Trench Mortar Bty, and any other Units who may be with them.
Units will also arrange to get the Kits of all Officers & men up to theirs units by to-night.
Indents will also be submitted at once for Blankets & Great Coats.

4. Brigade Headquarters will move to RIBECOURT at about 4 pm.

5 Acknowledge

[illegible]
Captain
Brigade Major
86th Inf. Brigade

2/12/17.

6 Units (4). BC 26

The 86th Inf Brigade will withdraw from the area in which it is at present assembled and will withdraw to TRESCAULT after dusk tonight. Details of accommodation will be sent when received. Guides from Division will be at Road junction at R.36.c.1.1. from dusk onwards.

One officer per Battalion and one guide per Company will meet a representative of Brigade Staff at 2nd Royal Fusiliers Headquarters at 3 pm to reconnoitre the route to R.36.c.1.1: Battalions will march at the following times 2nd Royal Fusiliers 4-15 pm 1st Lancashire Fus. 4 30 pm 16th Middx Regt 4-45 pm 1st R.G.L.I. 5 pm Personnel of 86th M G Coy + T M Bty will march with Units to which they are attached. There will be an interval of 100 yards between companies on the march. One officer per Battalion should be sent at once to TRESCAULT to meet A/Staff Captain re arrange accommodation

[illegible] Captain

2/12/17

Brigade Major
86th Inf Brigade

Army Form C. 2121
(in pads of 100).

"A" Form
MESSAGES AND SIGNALS.

No. of Message..................

Prefix............Code..............m.	Words.	Charge.	This message is on a/c of:	Recd. at...........m.
Office of Origin and Service Instructions.	Sent		...........................Service.	Date..................
	At..............m.			From..................
	To..................			
	By..................		(Signature of "Franking Officer.")	By..................

TO { 6 Units. (5)

Sender's Number.	Day of Month.	In reply to Number.	AAA
* BC 24.	3/12		

Warning Order AAA Orders are expected shortly to move to somewhere in the neighbourhood of EQUANCOURT AAA In this event the move will take place by day the troops moving in small formed bodies of about 50 strong each with an Officer AAA There will be an interval of 200 yards between each party AAA There must be no straggling and the strictest march discipline maintained AAA A "slow squad" will be formed in each Battalion for those who are not able to keep up. AAA There will be an Officer with this party

From
Place
Time

The above may be forwarded as now corrected. (Z)

Censor. Signature of Addressor or person authorised to telegraph in his name.

* This line should be erased if not required.

(18965.) Wt. W12952/M1294. 187,500 Pads. 1/17 McC. & Co., Ltd. (E. 818.)

(6)

86th INFANTRY BRIGADE ORDER No.195.

1. Reference attached copy of 29th Division Order No.22 Batta lions w ill move in accordance with attached March Table.

2. All Units leaving to-morrow are to play their Bands marching t o the entraining station.

3. Transport will move in a ccordance w ith attached 29th Division Order, Transport moving by Road will be under orders of Lie ut. HAMILTON, 2/Royal Fusiliers who will be responsible to O.C, Div. Train, Transport moving by Rail will be under orders of Lieut. COOK, 16/Middlesex Regt. and will comence to move from W.13.b. at 8.30 a.m.

4. Breakfasts will be arranged so that Cookers can move at 8 a.m.

5. Units will detail a representative to take over rations for consumption 6th instant at ETRICOURT on the 5th instant at 9 a.m.

6. Billeting parties will report to Staff Captain at detraining station for instructions.

7. Guides from Battalions for Lor ries to report to Acting Staff Captain at Division H.Q. at SOR EL at 5 a.m. Guides from M.G.Coy. and T.M.Bty., report at Brigade H.Q. at 9 a.m.

8. Marching out statements to be rendered to this office by 9 a.m. to-morrow.

9. A C K N O W L E D G E.

Captain,
A/Brigade Major,
86th Infantry Brigade.

4th December, 1917.

S E C R E T.

29th DIVISION ADMINISTRATIVE ORDER No. 22.

1. The 29th Division, less Royal Artillery and 1/2nd Monmouth Regt, will move to LE CAUROY Area, by road and rail on 5.12.17 in accordance with attached Table "A".

2. Transport less that portion moving ny rail (see attached Table "B") will move by march route under O.C., Divisional Train.
All Transport not moving by rail will assemble at a time and place to be selected by O.C., Divisional Train, and march under his orders as follows:-

1st Stage.............. BAPAUME.
2nd Stage .... COUTURELLE (9 miles East of DOULLENS)

From COUTURELLE Transport will march to Units Billets in new area. Instructions will be sent to O.C., Divisional Train at COUTURELLE on the 6th instant as to billets.
S.A.A. Section will accompany this Transport.

3. Time table of Transport moving by rail is laid down in attached Table "A".

4. (a) Blankets, greatcoats and camp kettles are to be collected into dumps by Brigades as follows:-

86th Brigade ..... FINS.
87th Brigade ..... SOREL
88th Brigade...... as detailed in (b)

(b.) Blankets of 88th Brigade, now on Transport, must be dumped at old 88th Brigade Store, SOREL, to be picked up there (with those now in the store) by lorries detailed below in para. (c).

(c) Eleven lorries will report at Divisional Headquarters, SOREL, at 5 a.m. on the 5th instant to move these blankets etc. to entraining station for loading on to railway train.

Lor
87 Bde 4
86 - 4
88 - 3

(d) If necessary lorries must do a double journey. Brigades will send guides to meet their Lorries at Divisional Headquarters at 5 a.m.

(e) Six lorries will be provided at detraining station for each Brigade. These must do double journeys if necessary.

5 (a) Rations for consumption on the 5th are being delivered to Transport Lines, J.13.b., for 86th and 87th Brigades and to ETRICOURT Station at 9.a.m. for 88th Bde.

(b) Rations for consumption on the 6th are being delivered to ETRICOURT (entraining Station) by Divisional Train on the morning of the 5th instant. Units must arrange for a representative to take them over at 9 a.m. to report to R.T.O. Office.ETRICOURT.

(c) Rations for consumption on the 7th instant will be delivered in new area by Divisional Supply Column.

(d) Two days forage for horses and rations for personnel of transport moving by rail will be delivered at BAPAUME Station at 12.00 on the 5th instant. Brigade Transport Officers must arrange for a representative to ride on ahead and take it over.

(e) Forage and rations of Transport moving by road will be delivered by Divisional Train en route.

(f) All transport and horses not detailed to proceed by rail in Table B must proceed by road under O.C., Divisional Train.

P.T.O.

6 Headquarter Company Divisional Train will be located at 29th Divisional Ammunition Column Lines, V.3.c., (ETRICOURT) and will proceed there under orders of O.C., Divisional Train on morning of the 5th instant. Supply Vehicles for Pioneers must be attached to this Company.

7. Instructions as to Units' Billets will be given at detraining station.

8. Divisional Headquarters will be at LE CAUROY.

Lieut. Colonel,
A.A. & Q.M.G., 29th Division.

4th November 1917.

Copies

86th Brigade	10	Signals	1
87th Brigade	10	227 M.G.Co.	1
88th Brigade	10	III Corps	1
C.R.E.	4	IV Corps	1
C.R.A.	1		
A.D.M.S.	4		
D.A.D.V.S.	1		
Supply Col.	1		
D.A.D.O.S.	1		
A.P.M.	1		
Div. Train	5		
S.S.O.	1		
1/2nd Mons.	1		
G.S.	2		
Camp Cmdt.	1		
Employt. Co.	1		
S.A.A. Section	1		

Attach'd to HQ 86 Sdy
Bde
Dupl July to Dec 17

ARMY POST

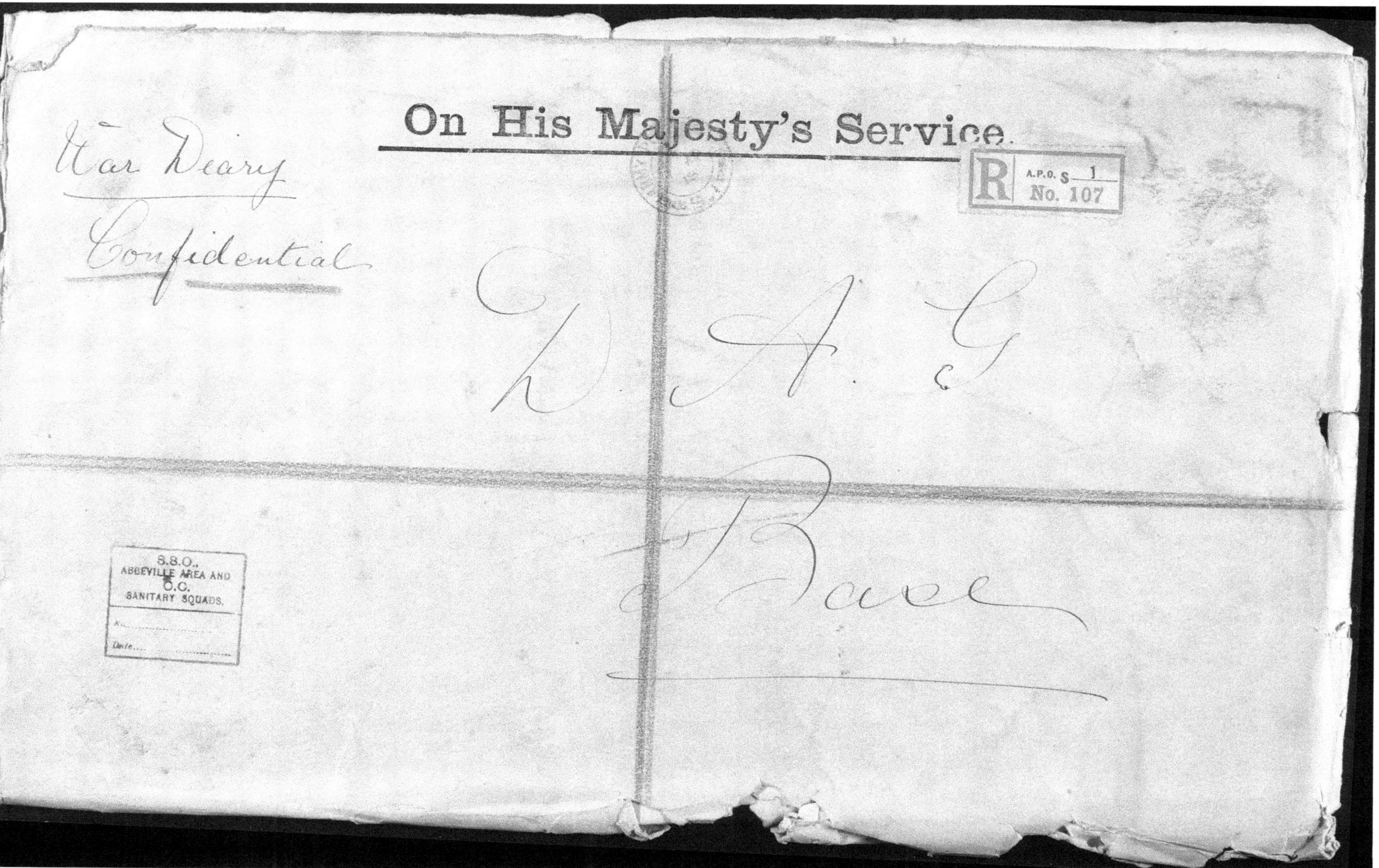
War Diary

Confidential

On His Majesty's Service.

R A.P.O. S 1 No. 107

D. A. G.

Base

S.S.O.,
ABBEVILLE AREA AND
O.C.
SANITARY SQUADS.

Date....

Duplicate

WAR DIARY
for
JULY 1917

86 TM Bty
Dup July to Dec 17
to be attached to
86 Infy Bde

86TH
TRENCH MORTAR
BATTERY.

No. B 92.
Date 6.4.18

To D.A.G
3rd Echelon
Base.

Herewith please find Duplicate Copies of WARDIARIES for JULY, AUGUST, SEPTEMBER, OCTOBER, NOVEMBER, and DECEMBER, 1917 as per instructions laid down in G.R.O. 1598.

J S Lawson
Captain
O.C. 86TH T.M. BATTERY

Army Form C. 2118.

Instructions regarding War Diaries and Intelligence Summaries are contained in F. S. Regs., Part II. and the Staff Manual respectively. Title Pages will be prepared in manuscript.

WAR DIARY
or
INTELLIGENCE SUMMARY
(Erase heading not required.)

Place	Date	Hour	Summary of Events and Information	Remarks and references to Appendices
HAANDEKOT B.1.F 27 N.E.	5/7/17	14.00	The battery marched to PROVEN AREA No 2 & was accomodated in tents & billets (F.9.a.5.9 1/20,000 27 N.E.	
	6/7/17		Strength reduced from 53 to 52 (1 Bdr admitted Hospital (V)	
	11/7/17		During the above period training was carried out daily, the weather fine warm	
PROVEN AREA No 2	12/7/17	18.15	No 1 Section marched to CORRIDOR TR, ZWANOF SECTOR & relieved the 88th T.M.B.	
	13/7/17	14.00	No 1 Section (1/2 Hide) relieved 88th T.M.B in BAIRD TR, HUDDLESTONE TR & NIKE TR (1/2 Hide)	
ZWANOF SECTOR		18.00	No 2 Section relieved remaining half of 88 T.M.B in CORRIDOR TR. Relief was carried out during daylight & was completed by 19.00 (Map Ref St Julien 28 N.W.2 1/10,000 C.13)	
	15/7/17	02.00	CEASERS NOSE bombarded * great damage was done duckboards & other debris were seen flying in all directions * (Guns in HUDDLESTONE TR)	
	17/7/17	16.30	No 2 Section (CORRIDOR TR) relieved No 1 section in front system, relief carried out during daylight & completed by 17.00	
	18/7/17		BOMbardment commenced, Royal Fusiliers raided C.8.b.8.9 (6 Prisoners) NEWFOUNDLAND Regt & 1st Border Regt raided enemy trenches at C.7.d 28.70, C.13.b 90.78	
	18/7/17	21.00	A heavy barrage was put down on the enemy's trenches in response to S.O.S sent up by division on our right. Heavy enemy retaliation. Heavy casualties amongst regt holding line	
	19/7/17		bombardment increased, enemy retaliation slight, weather during day unsettled	[illegible]

Army Form C. 2118.

Instructions regarding War Diaries and Intelligence Summaries are contained in F. S. Regs., Part II. and the Staff Manual respectively. Title Pages will be prepared in manuscript.

WAR DIARY
or
INTELLIGENCE SUMMARY

(Erase heading not required.)

Place	Date	Hour	Summary of Events and Information	Remarks and references to Appendices
ZWANOF SECTOR	19/7/17	14.00	No 1 Section relieved by 38th DIV proceed to H CAMP	
	20/7/17	01.00	1st R.I.B. raided enemy trenches at C.7.a 60.75 no prisoners	Attached Orders
			Slight enemy retaliation, 1 Gun Pit in HUDDLESTONE TR partially destroyed 1 gun put out of action	
	21/7/17	15.00	Remainder of battery relieved by 38th DIV. Relief was completed by 16.00. ~~[illegible]~~ CORPS STAGING	
		09.00	Two Sections moved to ~~[illegible]~~ AREA ~~[illegible]~~	
			During this tour the weather was good, there were no casualties. At times enemy shelling was very heavy, several emplacements were partially destroyed & amount of work entailed considerable	
			From 21/7/17 to 23/7/17 Parades training were carried out as usual.	
	24/7/17		The battery moved to PROVEN AREA No 3 & relieved the 88 T.M.B.	
			One N.C.O & 6 men were temporarily attached to each battalion for the forthcoming operations, it was decided to allot each battalion 1 gun 6 mules & 1 G.S. wagon mules & wagons were supplied by the D.A.C. These guns were to be controlled entirely by battalion commanders (One officer will probably be attached to [each] two battalions	
	25/7/17	08.30	Field day (Officers only attended) remainder of battery training as usual	Orders Attached
	26/7/17		Training as usual	
	27/7/17	08.30	Field day (Officers only attended)	

2449 Wt. W14957/M90 750,000 1/16 J.B.C. & A. Forms/C.2118/12.

Army Form C. 2118.

Instructions regarding War Diaries and Intelligence Summaries are contained in F. S. Regs., Part II. and the Staff Manual respectively. Title Pages will be prepared in manuscript.

WAR DIARY
or
INTELLIGENCE SUMMARY
(Erase heading not required.)

Place	Date	Hour	Summary of Events and Information	Remarks and references to Appendices
PROVEN AREA No 3	26-7-17 to 30/7/17		Battery training as usual	
	30/7/17	00.15	The battery relieves the 87 T.M.B in PROVEN AREA No 2. Weather wet & misty but the att[illegible] was reduced to a minimum. Surplus sent to DUMP under Brigade arrangements. Strength increased from 48 to 64. Reserve personnel attached for duty. Brigade under 3 hours notice to move	
XIV Corps Front		10.00	Advance commences.	
		10.50	Situation — 1 Guards Brigade believed to be from Railway U 27 b 4.6 along western bank to U 21 d.4.2. over Steenbeek opposite ROISSEAU Fm. Line definitely reported along green line. Firm in touch with FRENCH on green line at U 20 c 5.7. Prisoners 11 off 237 OR unwounded. War material captured not reported	Maps Ref LANGEMARCK 1/10000
		11.30	Hostile counter attack made on 38 DIV. at AU BON GITE U 18 central completely smashed by Artillery, rifle & M.G fire. Some prisoners taken from assaulting troops	

2449 Wt. W14957/M90 750,000 1/16 J.B.C. & A. Forms/C.2118/12.

DIARY
for July 1917
H.T.M.B.

Duplicate

WAR DIARY

for

AUGUST 1917

Army Form C. 2118.

Instructions regarding War Diaries and Intelligence Summaries are contained in F. S. Regs., Part II. and the Staff Manual respectively. Title Pages will be prepared in manuscript.

WAR DIARY
or
INTELLIGENCE SUMMARY
(Erase heading not required.)

Place	Date	Hour	Summary of Events and Information	Remarks and references to Appendices
PROVEN Area No 2	1/8/17		Heavy rain for 24 hours. Strength ~~[illegible]~~ [illegible] 1 NCO and two 1 OR returned to battalion — 69	
	2/8/17	08.30	3 hours notice cancelled. Total prisoners captured by 5th Army 130 off 5780 OR. by [illegible] 772 O.R. - wounded 20 off 2441 OR one 10.5cm How, 11 M.G., 29 T.M. & 2 L.T.M.	
			Continued rain	
	3/8/17	15.30	Relieved 8th T.M.B in ~~S~~ FOREST Area Camp A.4.d.9.3 (Ref 28.N.W BELGIUM 1/20,000). Bivouacs, tent-hut. Very muddy conditions & continued rain.	
FOREST AREA.	4/8/17		Continued rain	
	5/8/17		Weather conditions considerably improved — no rain. Slight enemy shelling of this area with long range guns. One man leave — one L/Cpl evacuated — Strength 66	
			Bombs were dropped in this area during the night	
	6/8/17	14.45	Bombs dropped by hostile aeroplanes. Weather still good	
	7/8/17		Weather still good	
		21-00	Heavy gun fire was heard, the barrage lasted until about 22.15	
	8/8/17	19.00	Weather showery	
	9/8/17	19.00	Camp moved to A5c5.2 Weather good	
	10/8/17	~~[illegible]~~	Weather good	
	11/8/17		Enemy shelled vicinity of [illegible] Brigade Headquarters Camp A4d.9.3. from 22 with long range guns. Orders received 11am to take 4 guns to support 16th MIDDLESEX in their	

2449 Wt. W14957/M90 750,000 1/16 J.B.C. & A. Forms/C.2118/12.

August 1917
86th T.M.B.

Instructions regarding War Diaries and Intelligence Summaries are contained in F. S. Regs., Part II. and the Staff Manual respectively. Title Pages will be prepared in manuscript.

WAR DIARY
or
INTELLIGENCE SUMMARY
(Erase heading not required.)

Army Form C. 2118.

Place	Date	Hour	Summary of Events and Information	Remarks and references to Appendices
FOREST AREA	11/8/17	11.00	Attack on PASSERELLE FARM U11.c.42.95 (Ref. BIXSCHOOTE 20.S.W.4 1/10000). Capt. J. Blair White went up to reconnoitre returning 15.30.	
		18.00	Battery proceeded up the line. Capt. J. Blair White. Lieut. H. Layer, 2nd Lt. A.G. Killingly. Heavy thunderstorm 21.30.	
LANGEMARCK – BOESINGHE Sector.	12/8/17	00.15.	On reaching CAPTAINS FARM U26.b.20.65 (Ref. LANGEMARCK 1/10000) the Battery was caught in a heavy hostile artillery barrage, suffering heavy casualties. (KILLED 3. O.R. DIED OF WOUNDS 2. WOUNDED 1.O (Lieut. H. Layer) 3 O.R.). Battery obliged to withdraw.	
FOREST AREA		5.00	Battery returned to camp. Roads bad. Tracks from Advanced Bde HQ very muddy and cut up making progress slow. Weather showery.	
	13/8/17		Weather unsettled.	
	14/8/17	3.15	Enemy shelling this area with long range guns (1 O.R. KILLED). Received orders to hand over 1 Stokes Gun & team to each Batt. Received Brigade Order that 29th Division in conjunction with troops on Right & Left will renew the attack, time to be notified later. Weather showery.	attached order / attached order
	15/8/17	2.00	Received orders that one of officers to accompany each of the Stokes Guns attached to 2nd Royal Fusiliers & 1st R.D.F. Regiment	attached order
		12.30	Capt. J. Blair White went to join gun team attached to 1st R.D.F.	
		16.00	2nd Lt. A.G. Killingly went to join gun team attached to 2nd R.F.	
		"	Received Brigade Order 163. reference attack 86th Brigade	
		7.00	Received B.M.R. 26	attached order
	16/8/17.	4.45.	Zero. 29th Division attacked	attached order

2449 Wt. W14957/M90 750,000 1/16 J.B.C. & A. Forms/C.2118/12.

Army Form C. 2118.

WAR DIARY
or
INTELLIGENCE SUMMARY
(Erase heading not required.)

Instructions regarding War Diaries and Intelligence Summaries are contained in F. S. Regs., Part II. and the Staff Manual respectively. Title Pages will be prepared in manuscript.

Place	Date	Hour	Summary of Events and Information	Remarks and references to Appendices
FOREST AREA	16/8/17	12.15	Received news that the Trench objective has been captured in its entire length. Weather good.	Attached.
	Night of 16/17/8/17		86th Brigade + 1 Battn. 87th Brigade take over new line from 87th + 88th Brigades.	Attached order
	17		Weather good	
	18	19.15	Capt. [illegible] White wounded. Hostile aircraft active over back areas. Bombs were dropped. Weather good.	
		21.00		
	Night of 19/20/8/17		Lan. Fus. + [illegible] Regt. came out of the line. 2 men of Lan. Fus. were missing from out of action. Weather still good.	
	20	3.00	[illegible] Killingley) 2 O.R. wounded. Heavy shelling on front system. Weather good	
	Night of 20/21/8/17		4th R.D.F. and 2 R.F. relieved.	
	21/8/17		Weather good	
	22/8/17	21.00 to 21.30	Hostile aircraft active. Bombs were dropped on FOREST AREA. Weather good.	
	23/8/17		Gun team attached to Battn. join the Battery.	
	24/8/17		Weather good.	
	25/8/17	10 a.m.	1 officer (2/Lt. B[illegible] 2 R.F.) and 9 O.R. taken on strength to replace casualties. 3 O.R. (attached returned to units being incompetent) Weather good.	

Army Form C. 2118.

Instructions regarding War Diaries and Intelligence Summaries are contained in F. S. Regs., Part II. and the Staff Manual respectively. Title Pages will be prepared in manuscript.

WAR DIARY
or
INTELLIGENCE SUMMARY

(Erase heading not required.)

Place	Date	Hour	Summary of Events and Information	Remarks and references to Appendices
FOREST AREA	26/8/17		Weather good.	
	27/8/17		Weather unsettled	
PROVEN AREA (P3)	28/8/17		1st Division relieved by the Guards Division in the LEFT SECTOR.	
		11.00	[illegible] Brigade moved to PROVEN. P3 AREA. Battery accommodated in PITT CAMP (W.30.d.2.[illegible]) of map (Sheet 19.S.E). Heavy rain	
	29/8/17		Work on Camp. Weather bad.	
	30/8/17		Resumed [illegible] training and Bde Sports. [illegible] Pte Healey [illegible] awarded Military Medal. Weather improved.	
	31/8/17		Weather better.	

2449 Wt. W14957/M90 750,000 1/16 J.B.C. & A. Forms/C.2118/12.

Duplicate

WAR DIARY

for

SEPTEMBER

1917

Instructions regarding War Diaries and Intelligence Summaries are contained in F. S. Regs., Part II, and the Staff Manual respectively. Title pages will be prepared in manuscript.

WAR DIARY
or
INTELLIGENCE SUMMARY.
(Erase heading not required.)

Army Form C. 2118.

Place	Date	Hour	Summary of Events and Information	Remarks and references to Appendices
PROVEN. P3 AREA	1/9/17		Weather good.	
PITT CAMP	2/9/17		Weather good	
	3/9/17		1 Officer (2nd Lt N. SLOAN R.G.A.) taken on strength of Battery. Weather still good	
	4/9/17	11am	Brigade inspected by Divisional Commander. Presentation of honours awarded for services in the recent operations. No 21423 Pte J Healey (H.Q. attd. 8th T.M.B.) Military Medal. Weather very fine	Atts orders.
	5/9/17		Weather good. [illegible]	
	6/9/17		Weather good.	
	7/9/17		[illegible] Army School. Weather good.	
	8/9/17		Weather good. Hostile aeroplanes active at night over Back areas.	
	9/9/17		Weather still good. 1 O.R. struck off strength being evacuated to hospital.	
	10/9/17		Weather still good hostile aeroplanes active at night [illegible]	[illegible] A/Cam
	11/9/17		Weather good. The Brigade Sports in the afternoon.	
	12/9/17		Weather good.	
	13/9/17		1 O.R. taken on strength. 3 O.R. admitted to C.R.S.	

Army Form C. 2118.

Instructions regarding War Diaries and Intelligence Summaries are contained in F. S. Regs., Part II, and the Staff Manual respectively. Title pages will be prepared in manuscript.

WAR DIARY
or
INTELLIGENCE SUMMARY.
(Erase heading not required.)

Place	Date	Hour	Summary of Events and Information	Remarks and references to Appendices
PROVEN. P3 AREA	14/9/17		1 O.R. discharged from C.R.S. Weather good.	
	15/9/17		Weather good.	
HERZEELE	16/9/17		Battery moved to HERZEELE O.10.c.00.60 (Ref map BELGIUM–FRANCE 27.N.E 1/20000) in accordance with 11th Bde Order 170.	Att. Order
	17/9/17		Training at HERZEELE.	
	18/9/17		1 Gun team attached to each Battn to co-operate in training.	
	19/9/17	9 am	Brigade attack in accordance with 11th Bde Order No 172. 1 Gun team with each Battn, 2 guns in Brigade Reserve.	Att. Order
		15.00	Battery moved back to PROVEN. P3 AREA in accordance with 11th Bde Order No 174, arriving at Piot Camp 17.00.	[illegible]
PROVEN. P3 AREA		17.00	From the 28/5/17 to 19/9/17 Brigade shoots were organised in which the Battery took an active part	
WELLINGTON CAMP ([illegible])	20/9/17	17.00	Battery relieved 3rd Guards L.T.M.B in accordance with 11th Bde Order No 173 and 11th Bde Administrative Order No. 9. Battery accommodated in WELLINGTON CAMP 28.B.d.1.9 (Ref map BELGIUM 28.N.W). Movement by train	Att. orders
	21/9/17		Hostile aircraft active between 20.00 and 23.00. Weather good.	

D. D. & L., London, E.C.
(A7853) Wt W809/M1672 350,000 4/17 Sch 52a Forms/C/2118/14

Instructions regarding War Diaries and Intelligence Summaries are contained in F. S. Regs., Part II, and the Staff Manual respectively. Title pages will be prepared in manuscript.

WAR DIARY
or
INTELLIGENCE SUMMARY.
(Erase heading not required.)

Army Form C. 2118.

Place	Date	Hour	Summary of Events and Information	Remarks and references to Appendices
WELLINGTON CAMP	21/9/17		Battery engaged on work on camp. Weather good.	
	22/9/17		During the night vicinity of camp occasionally shelled with H.V. guns.	
			Work on the camp. Hostile aircraft active during the day.	
			1 officer 2/Lt Wingfield C.F. 11 RGA + 1 O.R. taken on strength. Weather good.	
	23/9/17		Work on TRACK. 11 & new drain with Bde Orders 6/11/19. For details to Brothers from B.9.c.0.2 to stream at B.8.d.7.2 (ref map BELGIUM. 28. N.W) Hostile aircraft active over this area 20.00 to 23.00. Weather good	M. orders
	24/9/17		Work on TRACK. 11. Weather good.	
	25/9/17		Work on TRACK 11. Hostile aircraft active in the evening over this area and vicinity. Weather good	
	26/9/17		Work on TRACK 11. Two O.R. taken on strength. Weather good	
	27/9/17		Work on TRACK 11. E.A. again active over this area. Bombs were dropped in the vicinity of ELVERDINGHE. Weather good	
	28/9/17	9.30	Working Party on TRACK 11.	
		7.15	Two gun teams under 2/Lt B. LIGHT left camp to report to C.O. 11 RDF.	

D. D. & L., London, E.C.
(A7883) Wt W829/M1672 350,000 4/17 Sch 52a Forms/C/2118/14

Instructions regarding War Diaries and Intelligence Summaries are contained in F. S. Regs., Part II, and the Staff Manual respectively. Title pages will be prepared in manuscript.

WAR DIARY
or
INTELLIGENCE SUMMARY.

(*Erase heading not required.*)

Army Form C. 2118.

Place	Date	Hour	Summary of Events and Information	Remarks and references to Appendices
WELLINGTON CAMP	1/11/17		at Batt H.Q. at U.22. C. 08. 10 (Ref map. BROEMBEEK 1/10000). Guns in position at U.23. A. 60.95 and U.23. B. 58.30 (Ref map BROEMBEEK 1/10000)	
	2/11/17		Worked on MARK 1b [redacted] [illegible] during the evening weather good. Two gun teams under 2/Lt SALAR went into the line & took up position at U.23 a. 60. 91 (Ref map. BROEMBEEK 1/10000).	
	3/11/17.		Weather good.	

D. D. & L., London, E.C.
(A7883) Wt W809/M1672 350,000 4/17 Sch 52a Forms/C/2118/14

Dapleeili

86TH
TRENCH MORTAR
BATTERY.
No.....................
Date...................

WAR DIARY
for
OCTOBER
1917

Instructions regarding War Diaries and Intelligence Summaries are contained in F. S. Regs., Part II, and the Staff Manual respectively. Title pages will be prepared in manuscript.

WAR DIARY
or
INTELLIGENCE SUMMARY.
(Erase heading not required.)

Army Form C. 2118.

Place	Date	Hour	Summary of Events and Information	Remarks and references to Appendices
WELLINGTON	1 Oct	2000	Two gun teams under 2/Lt. Wingfield relieved 2/Lt Light and two gun	
CAMP			teams in the line at U.23.a.60.90. (ref map M.1. [illegible]). Weather good	
	2		Battery in the line. Forward H.Q. at U.23.c.15.75 (ref map. BROEMBEEK 1/10000)	
	3.		Guns in line ranging on targets in accordance with Barrage scheme	[illegible]
			laid down by 56th Bde. Two gun teams under 2/Lt. [illegible] reported to	
	4.	2000	O.C. Right Company 1st R.D.F. [illegible] EAGLE TR. (U.23.b.60.30 (ref map	
			BROEMBEEK 1/10000) at midnight. Weather good.	
	4.		Zero Day. The two guns under 2/Lt LIGHT advanced behind [illegible]	
			[illegible] the 1st C.O.F. Remaining guns fired in accordance with	
			56th T.M.B. Barrage. 3 O.R. killed 1 [illegible] (2/Lt LIGHT) 3 O.R. wounded.	
	5.		In night 4/5th 56th Bde relieved by the [illegible]	
HARROW CAMP	6	1100	Battery relieved in WELLINGTON CAMP by 1st Guards Bde T.M.B. Battery	
			assembled in HARROW CAMP. Weather very bad.	
	7.	1600	2/Lt SHEAR and two gun teams went into the line with the	
			1st L.A. Position taken up at U.18.c.90.60 (ref map BROENBEEK 1/10000)	
	8.	1600	Battery moved to WHITE MILL CAMP (B.15.a.02.70. 28 NW 1/20000)	

D. D. & L., London, E.C.
(A7883) Wt W809/M1672 350,000 4/17 Sch 52a Forms/C/2118/14

Instructions regarding War Diaries and Intelligence Summaries are contained in F. S. Regs., Part II. and the Staff Manual respectively. Title pages will be prepared in manuscript.

WAR DIARY
or
INTELLIGENCE SUMMARY.
(Erase heading not required.)

Army Form C. 2118.

Place	Date	Hour	Summary of Events and Information	Remarks and references to Appendices
WHITE MILL CAMP	8/10/17	6 a.m.	Two gun teams under 2/Lt Wingfield went into the line at U.18.a.95.60. Forward Headquarters were at U.23.c.05.10. (ref map BROENBEEK Town) Weather bad.	All orders.
	9/10/17		ZERO DAY. Attack resumed by 29th Division in cooperation with [illegible] on right flank. Two gun teams under 2/Lt SAGAR advanced behind rear wave of 2nd [illegible] took up position at [illegible] HOUSES U.18.c.70.25 (ref map BROENBEEK Town). Casualties 1 O.R. killed 3 O.R. wounded. Battery relieved on the night of 9/10.	
PROVEN P.5 AREA	10.	9am	[illegible] Bde being relieved [illegible] in P.5 AREA. Battery accommodated in PRETORIA camp.	
	11		Weather unsettled.	
	12.		Weather unsettled.	
	13.		Battery inspected by G.O.C. Brigade. Weather still unsettled. Received warning order re move.	
	14.		Weather good.	
	15.		Received 86th Bde Order 183 re move. Weather good.	

D. D. & L., London, E.C.
(A7883) Wt W809/M1672 350,000 1/17 Sch 52a Forms/C/2118/14

Instructions regarding War Diaries and Intelligence Summaries are contained in F. S. Regs., Part II, and the Staff Manual respectively. Title pages will be prepared in manuscript.

WAR DIARY
or
INTELLIGENCE SUMMARY.
(Erase heading not required.)

Army Form C. 2118.

Place	Date	Hour	Summary of Events and Information	Remarks and references to Appendices
PRETORIA CAMP ~~P.5~~	16.10.17	12.25	Battery in accordance with 86th Bde. Order 183 entrained at HOUPOUTRE L.17.d (ref map. 27 NE France). Detrained at BEAUMETZ. Marched	Attd Ord
BLAIRVILLE	17.10.17	2.30	to No 2 camp BLAIRVILLE.	
CAMP No 2.	18.10.17		Court of Inquiry held to enquire into the alleged absence and deficiencies of kit of No. 3311 Pte Robinson S. 1st L.R. Weather very good.	
	19.10.17		Improving camp. 1 Officer (2/Lt WINGFIELD) and 9 O.R. left Battery to rejoin 1st R.D.F.	
	20.10.17		1 Officer (Lt MARTIN) and 11 O.R. from 1st R.G.L.I. 1 Officer (2/Lt WATTS) and 4 O.R. from 2nd R.F. 6 O.R. from 16th Middlesex Regt taken on strength of Battery. 3 O.R. to Rest camp. Weather good	
	21.10.17.		Weather fine	
	22.10.17.		Training in accordance with attached programme. 1 O.R. leave to England. Capt S.R. Hinde four days rest at No CONVALESCENT CAMP.	
	23.10.17.		Training. Weather bad.	

D. D. & L., London, E.C.
(A7883) Wt W809/M1672 350,000 4/17 Sch 52a Forms/C/2118/14

Army Form C. 2118.

WAR DIARY
or
INTELLIGENCE SUMMARY.
(Erase heading not required.)

Instructions regarding War Diaries and Intelligence Summaries are contained in F. S. Regs., Part II, and the Staff Manual respectively. Title pages will be prepared in manuscript.

Place	Date	Hour	Summary of Events and Information	Remarks and references to Appendices
BEHARVILLE	24.10.17		Training. Weather bad.	
Camp H.2.	25.10.17.		Weather very bad.	
	26.10.17	10.00	Brigade Ceremonial parade. Weather improved.	
	27.10.17	10.00	Brigade Ceremonial parade. Weather improved.	
	28.10.17.		1 Officer ([illegible]) + 7 O.R. admitted to hospital. Weather good	

D. D. & L., London, E.C.
(A7853) Wt W809/M1672 350,000 4/17 **Sch 52a** Forms/C/2118/14

Diary for October 1917

Duplicate

86TH
TRENCH MORTAR
BATTERY.

No.........................

Date......................

WAR DIARY

for

NOVEMBER

1917

Instructions regarding War Diaries and Intelligence Summaries are contained in F. S. Regs., Part II. and the Staff Manual respectively. Title Pages will be prepared in manuscript.

WAR DIARY
or
INTELLIGENCE SUMMARY
(Erase heading not required.)

Army Form C. 2118.

Place	Date	Hour	Summary of Events and Information	Remarks and references to Appendices
BLAIRVILLE Camp No. 2	1/11/17		Training. Showery. 1 OR from Hospital. 3 OR from Rest Camp.	
	2/11/17		Training. Brigade Practice Ceremonial Parade for the presentation of	
		1500	Medals. Battery awarded 1 MC [illegible] 1 DCM 2 MM [illegible]	
			Weather fair.	
	3/11/17		Training. 1 OR to Hospital. Weather [illegible]	
	4/11/17		Weather fair	
	5/11/17		Training.	
		1430	Cross Country Competition. Weather good.	
	6/11/17		Training. [illegible] OR on strength of Battery. 1 OR Returned to Unit unfit for T.M. work.	
	7/11/17		Training. Weather showery.	
	8/11/17		Training. Weather fair.	
	9/11/17		Training. Weather fair.	
	10/11/17		Training. Weather showery. 1 Officer returned from Hospital.	
	11/11/17		Weather improved.	
	12/11/17		Training. 1 OR to Hospital. Received Bde [illegible]	
	13/11/17	7.00	Brigade Tactical Exercise. [illegible]	
			each Battalion.	
	14/11/17	7.00	Brigade Tactical exercise as before. Received Bde Operation Instructions [illegible]	attd.
	15/11/17	7.00	[illegible] tactical exercise. Guns and [illegible]	

2449 Wt. W14957/M90 750,000 1/16 J.B.C. & A. Forms/C.2118/12.

Instructions regarding War Diaries and Intelligence Summaries are contained in F. S. Regs., Part II. and the Staff Manual respectively. Title Pages will be prepared in manuscript.

WAR DIARY
or
INTELLIGENCE SUMMARY
(Erase heading not required.)

Army Form C. 2118.

Place	Date	Hour	Summary of Events and Information	Remarks and references to Appendices
BLAIREVILLE [illegible]	[illegible]/11/17		5 OR. To III Corps School for T. M. [illegible]	
	1[illegible]/11/17		Training. Weather bad. Preparation for move	
	[illegible]/11/17	21.30	Left BLAIREVILLE for [illegible] [illegible]ONENT where the Battery entrained for PERONNE at	attached order
			[illegible] PERONNE was reached at about 6.30 and marched to HAUT-ALLAINE where	
			it was accom[illegible] [illegible] huts with the [illegible] M.G. Coy.	
HAUT-ALLAINE	[illegible]/11/17	19.15	Battery marched from HAUT-ALLAINE to EQUANCOURT [illegible] reached	[illegible]
			about 00.30.	[illegible]
			Received [illegible] Order No 168.	[illegible]
EQUANCOURT	[illegible]/11/17	2.30	Battery [illegible] Gun Teams [illegible] attached [illegible] moved into position with	
			Brigade Reserve ready for the attack. Zero hour 6.20 x 3 hours.	
			Advance was very successful. Casualties 2 Off: Wounded [illegible]	
			Lieut F MARTIN took over command of Battery in place of Capt HIDE	
			wounded. Battery [illegible] H.Q. marched to VILLIERS PLOUCH	
VILLIERS PLOUICH	[illegible]/11/17	19.00	Battery [illegible] H.Q. [illegible] with Brigade to MARCOING where we joined the [illegible] Reserve	
MARCOING	2[illegible]/11/17		Gun Teams. Enemy Artillery below normal.	
			[illegible] ammunition and [illegible]	
	2[illegible]/11/17	22.3[illegible]	[illegible] MARCOING for MASNIERES where [illegible]	
MASNIERES	2[illegible]/11/17		Enemy Artillery very active. Had 9 Guns in line [illegible] [illegible] M.G.	
"	2[illegible]/11/17		Enemy artillery and Machine [illegible] active.	
	2[illegible]/11/17	[illegible].00	Enemy [illegible] [illegible] [illegible] throughout good.	

2449 Wt. W14957/M90 750,000 1/16 J.B.C. & A. Forms/C.2118/12.

Instructions regarding War Diaries and Intelligence Summaries are contained in F. S. Regs., Part II. and the Staff Manual respectively. Title Pages will be prepared in manuscript.

WAR DIARY
or
INTELLIGENCE SUMMARY
(Erase heading not required.)

Army Form C. 2118.

Place	Date	Hour	Summary of Events and Information	Remarks and references to Appendices
MASNIERES	27/11/17	2.00	Gun attached to first Lancashire Fusiliers had a premature [illegible] which wounded 2. O.R.	
		18.30	2nd Gun was blown up by enemy shell fire. (Command [illegible] Battery transferred to 2/Lt SAGAR N (1st Lancashire Fusiliers)). Received orders to fire at least 200 rounds per night. Orders duly carried out	
	28/11/17		Two O.R. wounded [illegible]. Gun positions heavily shelled.	
	29/11/17		1. Gun put out of action by enemy shell fire. 2 O.R. wounded.	
	30/11/17	8.00	Enemy opened intense bombardment and counter-attacked getting a footing into Les Rues Vertes. Capturing one ammunition dump which was later they were driven off. All we established 3 guns in close proximity. 1 O.R. Killed 4 O.R. wounded.	

2449 Wt. W14957/M90 750,000 1/16 J.B.C. & A. Forms/C.2118/12.

WAR DIARY
for
NOVEMBER
1917

Duplicate

86TH
TRENCH MORTAR
BATTERY.

No.........................

Date..................

WAR DIARY

for

DECEMBER

1917

Instructions regarding War Diaries and Intelligence Summaries are contained in F. S. Regs., Part II, and the Staff Manual respectively. Title pages will be prepared in manuscript.

WAR DIARY
or
INTELLIGENCE SUMMARY.
(Erase heading not required.)

Army Form C. 2118.

Place	Date	Hour	Summary of Events and Information	Remarks and references to Appendices
MASNIERES	1/12/17		We had 3 guns at the dump in LES RUES VERTES and fired about 30	
			[illegible] guns [illegible] driven out after severe fighting.	
		11.30	Enemy [illegible] in LES RUES VERTES	
		[illegible]	[illegible] received evacuation [illegible] from 86th Brigade. We had 2 guns	
			at the dump in LES RUES VERTES [illegible]	
			[illegible] remaining gun was [illegible] before evacuation	
			[illegible] stretchers [illegible] evacuation [illegible]	
			[illegible] orders to evacuate.	
			[illegible] BROWN LINE. [illegible]	
			[illegible] casualties during the operations were 2 O.R. killed	
			2 [illegible] and 16 O.R. wounded and [illegible] O.R. missing.	
			[illegible] Brigade to withdraw from BROWN LINE	
		[illegible]	[illegible] from [illegible]	
			to TRESCAULT after dusk.	
			[illegible] reached TRESCAULT [illegible]	
			[illegible] of 16th Mx Regt [illegible]	
			[illegible] belonging to the Battalion [illegible]	
			[illegible] evening.	

Army Form C. 2118.

Instructions regarding War Diaries and Intelligence Summaries are contained in F. S. Regs., Part II, and the Staff Manual respectively. Title pages will be prepared in manuscript.

WAR DIARY
or
INTELLIGENCE SUMMARY.

(Erase heading not required.)

Place	Date	Hour	Summary of Events and Information	Remarks and references to Appendices
			[illegible]	
[illegible]	[illegible]	[illegible]	[illegible]	
[illegible]	[illegible]	[illegible]	[illegible]	
[illegible]	[illegible]	[illegible]	[illegible]	
	[illegible]	[illegible]	[illegible]	

D. D. & L., London, E.C.
(A7883) Wt W809/M1672 350,000 4/17 Sch 52a Forms/C/2118/14

Instructions regarding War Diaries and Intelligence Summaries are contained in F. S. Regs., Part II, and the Staff Manual respectively. Title pages will be prepared in manuscript.

WAR DIARY
or
INTELLIGENCE SUMMARY.
(Erase heading not required.)

Army Form C. 2118.

Place	Date	Hour	Summary of Events and Information	Remarks and references to Appendices
[illegible]	[illegible]		[illegible]	

D. D. & L., London, E.C.
(A7883) Wt W809/M672 350,000 4/17 Sch 52a Forms/C/2118/14

Army Form C. 2118.

Instructions regarding War Diaries and Intelligence Summaries are contained in F. S. Regs., Part II, and the Staff Manual respectively. Title pages will be prepared in manuscript.

WAR DIARY
or
INTELLIGENCE SUMMARY.

(Erase heading not required.)

Place	Date	Hour	Summary of Events and Information	Remarks and references to Appendices
	[illegible]		[illegible]	
	[illegible]		Training. Weather [illegible]	
	[illegible]		[illegible]	
	[illegible]		Training	
	[illegible]		Xmas Day	
	[illegible]			
	28-29	[illegible]	Training 1 O.R. from Hospital	
	30		1 O.R. from Hospital 1 O.R. to Hospital	

D. D. & L., London, E.C.
(A7883) Wt W829/M1672 350,000 4/17 Sch 52a Forms/C/2118/14

Copy.

WAR DIARY.
for
DECEMBER
1917

86TH T.M. BATTERY

WAR DIARY

for

JANUARY

1918

86TH
TRENCH MORTAR
BATTERY.

No. War Diary

Date 31/1/18

Instructions regarding War Diaries and Intelligence Summaries are contained in F. S. Regs., Part II. and the Staff Manual respectively. Title pages will be prepared in manuscript.

WAR DIARY

~~or~~

~~INTELLIGENCE SUMMARY.~~

(Erase heading not required.)

Army Form C. 2118.

Place	Date	Hour	Summary of Events and Information	Remarks and references to Appendices
VERCHOCQ	1/1/18		Training Received 2nd Brigade Order No 197 re move. Weather very cold and snowy	
	2/1/18		Training. Registering, Firing, Signalling, Gas and examination of Box Respirators	
	3/1/18	0815	Battery moved into the TILQUES area in accordance with Brigade Order No 197 (att) Marched to ESQUERDES which was reached at 13.30 hours. Roads bad for marching and we were being held up continually by Transport of various other units. No one fell out. 1 O.R. leave to U.K. Billeted in 3 barns	197 (1)
ESQUERDES	4/1/18		Training weather warmer with thaw.	
	5/1/18		Training, practising barrage, 4 guns on strong point & then the 4 remaining guns putting up a barrage on E. communication trenches	
	6/1/18		Baths. 1 O.R on leave to U.K	
	7/1/18		Training 1 O.R on leave to U.K.	
	8/1/18		Ditto do } Weather cold and snowy	
	9/1/18		Ditto do	[illegible]

D. D. & L., London, E.C. (A7883) Wt W829/M672 350,000 4/17 Sch 52a Forms/C/2118/14

Army Form C. 2118.

Instructions regarding War Diaries and Intelligence Summaries are contained in F. S. Regs., Part II. and the Staff Manual respectively. Title pages will be prepared in manuscript.

WAR DIARY
or
~~INTELLIGENCE~~ SUMMARY.
(Erase heading not required.)

Place	Date	Hour	Summary of Events and Information	Remarks and references to Appendices
ECQUEDES	10/1/18		Brigade Practice Ceremonial Parade. Weather wet	
	11/1/18		Training etc. Received Brigade Order No 198 Weather Showery	
	12/1/18	11.30	Brigade Ceremonial Parade. Distribution of decorations by 29th Divisional Commander. March past. Battery went thro' gas chamber at 14.30 hours	
	13/1/18		March to Range 'C' for musketry. Received Brigade Order No 199. Weather still very cold and snowy	
	14/1/18	08.30	Brigade Tactical Exercise (Order 198 att.)	198 (2)
	15/1/18		2/Lieut E W PUTLAND, 16th Middlesex Regt and 2/Lieut A A MULLOY, 1st Royal Guernsey Light Infantry reported their arrival and were taken on the strength of the Battery. Cleaning up Billets etc & packing for move weather warmer	
	16/1/18	11.00	Moved by train to BRANDHOEK area in accordance with Brigade Order No 199 (att) Left WIZERNES station at 11.00 hours arrived BRANDHOEK at 13.30 hours and were accommodated in "B" Camp which was in a wretched condition. Received Brigade Order No 200	199 (3)
BRANDHOEK	17/1/18	14.45	March to ST JEAN preceded by C.O. who left at 6 hours in order	G.S.I. / 21

D. D. & L., London, E.C.
(A7883) Wt W809/M1672 350,000 4/17 Sch 52a Forms/C/2118/14

Instructions regarding War Diaries and Intelligence Summaries are contained in F. S. Regs., Part II. and the Staff Manual respectively. Title pages will be prepared in manuscript.

WAR DIARY

~~or INTELLIGENCE SUMMARY.~~

(*Erase heading not required.*)

Army Form C. 2118.

Place	Date	Hour	Summary of Events and Information	Remarks and references to Appendices
BRANDHOEK			to find out our dispositions in the area round PASSCHENDAELE RIDGE. arrived ST. JEAN 17.15 and were accommodated in tents at WELSH CAMP. Weather very wet.	200 (4)
WELSH CAMP	18/1/18		Received Brigade Order No. 201. Owing to bad condition of gun emplacements the T.M.B. not to go into the line but available for working parties. 8 O.c conference 11.00 hours. 4 O.R evacuated sick & struck off strength	207 (5)
		21.30	1 Officer and 20 O.R working party took up Trench Boards from GRAVENSTAFEL to BELLE VUE. This was accomplished by 05.00 19/1/18. Weather better	
	19/1/18		Improving camp by draining etc. 3 O.R wounded whilst at BILGE DUMP 15.15 hours	
		22.00	Working party of every available man to carry up Trench Boards and tape to BELLE VUE. This was accomplished and party returned to camp at 04.00. Weather favourable	
	20/1/18	16.00	2 Gun teams under 2/Lieut. Rutland went into the line Rest of Battery	

D. D. & L., London, E.C. (A7883) Wt W809/M1672 350,000 4/17 Sch 52a Forms/C/2118/14

Army Form C. 2118.

WAR DIARY
or
~~INTELLIGENCE SUMMARY.~~
(Erase heading not required.)

Instructions regarding War Diaries and Intelligence Summaries are contained in F. S. Regs., Part II. and the Staff Manual respectively. Title pages will be prepared in manuscript.

Place	Date	Hour	Summary of Events and Information	Remarks and references to Appendices
WELSH CAMP [redacted]			under 2/Lieuts Smith and Mulloy took up ammunition. The party returned at 09.00 hours 21/1/18. Track very muddy. Only shell hole positions possible & the 2 guns were placed at V.29.B.7.5 and V.29.A.8.4. Weather conditions very bad	
	21/1/18		Received Brigade Order No 202 dated 18/1/18. Weather improved	202 (6)
	22/1/18		2 Gun teams under 2/Lt Smith went up to relieve the teams under 2/Lt. Rutland in the line. Relief completed by 23.20 hours. Enemy shelling in back area. Weather showery	
	23/1/18		Draining Camp. Enemy still shelling back areas. Weather improved	
	24/1/18		2 Gun teams under 2/Lt Mulloy relieved the teams under 2/Lt Smith in the line. Relief completed by 23.00 hours. Enemy still shelling back areas	
	25/1/18		Men not in line improving camp. Received Brigade Order No 203. Weather fine. E.A. very active. No 415 Pte ENDRAUDEE.A. of 1st Royal Guernsey Lgt Infantry wounded on 19/1/18 died of wounds. Buried in 8th Corps Cemetery YPRES	203 (7)
				J.S.2 [illegible]

D. D. & L., London, E.C.
(A7883) Wt W8o9/M1672 350,000 4/17 Sch 52a Forms/C/2118/14

Instructions regarding War Diaries and Intelligence Summaries are contained in F. S. Regs., Part II. and the Staff Manual respectively. Title pages will be prepared in manuscript.

WAR DIARY

or

~~INTELLIGENCE SUMMARY.~~

(Erase heading not required.)

Army Form C. 2118.

Place	Date	Hour	Summary of Events and Information	Remarks and references to Appendices
WELSH CAMP	26/1/18		Battery relieved by 88th T.M.B. Moved to BRAKE CAMP in the BRANDHOEK area where we were accommodated in very comfortable huts. Relief completed by 01.30 hours 27/1/18. Weather very fine	
BRAKE CAMP	27/1/18		Resting, weather very fine	
	28/1/18		Reorganisation of Battery. Equipment, clothing etc checked. 1 OR in Hospital	
	29/1/18		Training etc. 1 OR from Hospital taken on strength. 1 OR on leave to U.K. in Hospital taken off strength.	
	30/1/18		Training. 1 Bar to Military Medal for Cambrai Operations for Battery. 1 OR in Hospital. Received Brigade warning order re move. Weather fine	
	31/1/18		Brigade Practice Ceremonial Parade. Weather fine but very cold. The following decorations were approved by 8th Corps Commander. Bar to Military Medal – No 22939 Pte Virgo T. 1st Lancashire Fusiliers	

D. D. & L., London, E.C. (A7883) Wt W809/M1672 350,000 4/17 Sch 52a Forms/C/2118/4

Army Form C. 2118.

Instructions regarding War Diaries and Intelligence Summaries are contained in F. S. Regs., Part II. and the Staff Manual respectively. Title pages will be prepared in manuscript.

WAR DIARY

~~or~~

~~INTELLIGENCE SUMMARY~~.

(Erase heading not required.)

Place	Date	Hour	Summary of Events and Information	Remarks and references to Appendices
			Decorations (continued)	
BRAKE CAMP	3/1/18		Military Medal	
			No 27257 Cpl. Cox E. W. } 2nd Royal Fusiliers	
			14372 L/Cpl Nicholls W } 2nd Royal Fusiliers	
			8614 Pte Mills A. } 1st Lancs. Fusiliers	
			23187 " Gill J } 1st Lancs. Fusiliers	
			J. S. Lawson Lieut. O.C. 86th T.M.B.	

D. D. & L., London, E.C. (A7283) Wt W859/M1672 350,000 4/17 Sch 52a Forms/C/2118/14

86 T.M.B

Instructions regarding War Diaries and Intelligence Summaries are contained in F. S. Regs., Part II. and the Staff Manual respectively. Title pages will be prepared in manuscript.

WAR DIARY
or
~~INTELLIGENCE SUMMARY.~~
(Erase heading not required.)

Army Form C. 2118.

Place	Date	Hour	Summary of Events and Information	Remarks and references to Appendices
BRANDOEK	1·2·18		Training etc. Weather V fine. Received Bde Order 204	
"	2·2·18		Preparing for move. Training continued. Weather still fine	
"	3·2·18		Battery moved to WELSH CAMP ST JEAN AREA as per Bde Instruction	
			Order 204 (att) Left BRAKE CAMP at 11·45 and proceeded by march route	I
			Arrived at WELSH CAMP at 14·15. Accomodated in 1 Hut and Bell	
			tents. Battery to be employed on salvage work while in this	
			area. 12 O.R. taken on strength. 1 O.R to Hospital Weather fine	
WELSH CAMP	4·2·18		Salvage work commenced. Plenty of material brought in. E Shelling	
			this area. E.A. V active. Weather Dry and Fine.	
"	5·2·18		Results of salvage work "good". Area again shelled. EA active	
			Weather still V fine	
"	6·2·18		A Party of 7 O.R proceeded to GRAVENSTAFEL under 2/LT SMITH	
			to bury dead. Left camp at 7·30 am and returned at 12.00 Noon	
			Remainder of Battery on salvage work. Medical Inspection for	
			all ranks. E A active. Weather fine. 1 O.R Hospital	
"	7·2·18		O.C. Battery went to PASCHENDAELE to reconnoitre part of line	E.W.P. 2/8

D. D. & L., London, E.C.
(A7853) Wt W8c9/M1672 350,000 4/17 Sch 52a Forms/C/2118/14

Instructions regarding War Diaries and Intelligence Summaries are contained in F. S. Regs., Part II. and the Staff Manual respectively. Title pages will be prepared in manuscript.

WAR DIARY

~~or~~

~~INTELLIGENCE SUMMARY.~~

(Erase heading not required.)

Army Form C. 2118.

Place	Date	Hour	Summary of Events and Information	Remarks and references to Appendices
WELSH CAMP	7-2-18		to be taken over. A party of 6 O.R under 2/LT SMITH salved 2 3" S.T.M	
"			Remainder of Battery proceeded under 2/LT E PUTLAND to CLUSTER HOUSES	
			D.7.D.7.7. to fetch Gas Cylinders which were emplaced on ridge.	
			19 Gas cylinders and 20 Projectors were got out under heavy shell	
			fire. These were brought down by train from NILE DUMP and taken	
			thence to VLAMERTINGHE to R.E DUMP. 1.O.R from hospital	
			Received 86th Bde warning order. Weather V Wet	
"	8-2-18		" " " Order 205 D/7-2-18. Salvage work continued. Party	II
			under 2/LT E. PUTLAND salved 72 Gas Projectors from CLUSTER HOUSES	
			1 Officer 1 O.R from Hospital. Weather still unfavourable.	
"	9-2-18		Received Bde Order. 206. Ref Relief. Battery continued on salvage work	III
			Weather fine	
"	10-2-18		Battery proceeded to D.7.D 77 to salve remainder Gas projectors Weather V fine.	
"	11-2-18		The Battery moved to POPERINGHE. Accomodated at 59 RUE D.YPRES with	
			H.Qs at 96 RUE D YPRES. 2 O.R remained at WELSH CAMP i/c of	E.W.P. 2/LT
			stores which could not be brought away owing to lack of transport.	
			Weather fine. 1.O.R leave to U.K.	

D. D. & L., London, E.C. (A7883) Wt W809/M1672 350,000 4/17 Sch 52a Forms/C/2118/14

Instructions regarding War Diaries and Intelligence Summaries are contained in F. S. Regs., Part II, and the Staff Manual respectively. Title pages will be prepared in manuscript.

WAR DIARY

~~or~~

~~INTELLIGENCE SUMMARY.~~

(*Erase heading not required.*)

Army Form C. 2118.

Place	Date	Hour	Summary of Events and Information	Remarks and references to Appendices
POPERINGHE	12-2-18		Battery occupied in cleaning Equipment. Checking Stores etc	
			attended Baths. S. B. Rs examined. 1 Officer 1 O.R leave to U K	
"	13-2-18		Training. Lecture "Trench Mortars" F. G. C. M. at H Qs at 10-45 am on 15013 Sgt G BETTRIDGE and 331 Sgt W. PAUL. The former N.C.O was acquitted. The latter was reduced to the ranks.	
			The C.O attended lecture by G. O. C Div at STEENVORDE. Weather "Wet."	
"	14-2-18		Training. Lectures. Weather "Showery" 1 O.R to Hospital 1 O.R to U.K. leave	
"	15-2-18		Training. Lectures. Baths. 2 O.R off strength to unit. Weather V cold but Bright	
"	16-2-18		Training. Received Bde Training Order. Weather V cold but fine.	
"	17-2-18		Lectures. "Stokes T.M in defence." "Gas" Received Bde Order 207 Ref Move IV. Weather Fine. but very cold.	
"	18-2-18		Training contd. 1 Officer (C.O) leave to U.K. 2/LT. E PUTLAND assumed temporary command of Battery. Preparing for move. Weather Fine.	
"	19-2-18		Battery moved from POPERINGHE at 9·10 am and left for EECKE by march route. Arrived EECKE area at 1.30 pm. Roads good. weather fine. Billeted in Barn at Q.15.B.3.4. Billets good.	E.W.P 2/Lt

D. D. & L., London, E.C.
(A7853) Wt W859/M1672 350,000 4/17 Sch 52a Forms/C/2118/14

Instructions regarding War Diaries and Intelligence Summaries are contained in F. S. Regs., Part II. and the Staff Manual respectively. Title pages will be prepared in manuscript.

WAR DIARY

~~or~~

~~INTELLIGENCE SUMMARY.~~

(Erase heading not required.)

Army Form C. 2118.

Place	Date	Hour	Summary of Events and Information	Remarks and references to Appendices
EECKE	20-2-18		Training. Lectures Recreation. Weather wet	
"	21-2-18		Training. Dummy Firing. "Gas" Lecture by B.G.O. Weather fine	
"	22-2-18		Training. Lectures. Dummy Firing. Visited by Commandant School of Cookery. C/O & attended conference of C.Os at B.H.Qs. Weather Dull	
"	23-2-18		Training Lectures Recreation. Weather fine. Received orders for C. Parade	
"	24-2-18		Church Parade. Weather fine.	
"	25-2-18		Training. Lecture to G.C.Os Recreation Weather fine.	
"	26-2-18		Practice Bde Ceremonial. 2 Officers 2 O.R attended lecture by the G.O.C. Division. Subject "Minor Tactics and Musketry Problems". 1 O.R to Hospital. 1 O.R from leave.	
"	27-2-18		Bde Ceremonial Parade. Inspection by G.O.C. Division. Weather fine. 1 Officer 1 O.R from leave.	
"	28-2-18		Firing at VIII Corps School for all ranks. Weather fine - Day. 1 O.R from leave. Received Defence Scheme of Army Battle Zone for VIII Corps area.	

E. Rutland 2/Lt.

D. D. & L., London, E.C.
(A7883) Wt. W809/M1672 350,000 4/17 Sch 52a Forms/C/2118/14

86TH
TRENCH MORTAR
BATTERY.

No.
Date 1.4.18

WAR DIARY

FOR

MARCH 1918

Instructions regarding War Diaries and Intelligence Summaries are contained in F. S. Regs., Part II, and the Staff Manual respectively. Title pages will be prepared in manuscript.

WAR DIARY
or
~~INTELLIGENCE SUMMARY.~~
(Erase heading not required.)

Army Form C. 2118.

Place	Date	Hour	Summary of Events and Information	Remarks and references to Appendices
EECKE	1-3-18		Training Lecture "Gas" Sports Weather fine but cold	
"	2-3-18		Training Continued. Drill. Exercise "Attack on M.G. Emplacements and Strong Points" Lecture "Review of above exercise. Weather cold Snow.	
	3-3-18		Training Cont'd Drill. March wearing S.B.Rs for 20 minutes Received Bde order No 208 Re Move. Weather cold. Wet	I attached
	4-3-18		Training contd. Drill. Baths. Received Bde orders Re Tactical exercise. Received Bde order to cancel same. Weather Wet & cold	
	5-3-18		Training contd. P.T and B.F. Lecture "Salvage" Sports Received Bde order re Tactical Exercise. Weather Bad. 2 O.R from U.K.	
	6-3-18		Bde Exercise. Battery marched from Starting Point at 12:30 1 Officer from leave to U.K. 1 Officer from course at Calais 1 O.R leave to U.K Weather fine.	
	7-3-18		Battery moved to BRANDHOEK. Left EECKE at 12·30 and proceeded to entraining point at GODEWAERSVELDE. Entrained at 14.00 and reached BRANDHOEK at 14.45. Accomodated	

D. D. & L., London, E.C.
(A7883) Wt W809/M.672 350,000 4/17 Sch 52a Forms/C/2118/14

Instructions regarding War Diaries and Intelligence Summaries are contained in F. S. Regs., Part II, and the Staff Manual respectively. Title pages will be prepared in manuscript.

WAR DIARY

or

~~INTELLIGENCE SUMMARY.~~

(Erase heading not required.)

Army Form C. 2118.

Place	Date	Hour	Summary of Events and Information	Remarks and references to Appendices
BRAKE CAMP			in BRAKE CAMP. 1 O.R leave to U.K. Weather Fine + Bright	
"	8-3-18		Training Drill etc. Weather Fine	
"	9-3-18		Battery on Salvage work. Results good. Weather Fine	
"	10-3-18		Baths 7 AM. Clothing and Blankets of men cleaned and disinfected	
"	11-3-18		Received wire from Bde stating that enemy was heavily shelling	
	"		our DIVISIONAL front. Prepared to move. Later Received Bde	
	"		wire cancelling orders re move. Received Bde Administration	
	"		order re Ceremonial Parade. Received Bde Order 22 re	
	"		move on 12th. Weather fine. 1 O.R leave to U.K.	
"	12-3-18		Battery moved to ST JEAN AREA. Left BRANDHOEK at 13.20	
	"		in accordance with Bde instructions. Arrived at WELSH CAMP	
	"		at 15-45. Were accomodated in 4 Bell Tents and part of	
	"		Nissen Hut. Weather fine.	
WELSH CAMP	13-3-18		Enemy shelling ST JEAN AREA. Battery on Salvage work and	
			preparing for duty in the front line. Weather fine and dry.	
	14-3-18		Battery moved up to front line to relieve the 88th T.M.B	

D. D. & L., London, E.C.
(A7883) Wt W809/M1672 350,000 4/17 Sch 52a Forms/C/2118/14

Instructions regarding War Diaries and Intelligence Summaries are contained in F. S. Regs., Part II, and the Staff Manual respectively. Title pages will be prepared in manuscript.

WAR DIARY
or
~~INTELLIGENCE SUMMARY.~~
(*Erase heading not required.*)

Army Form C. 2118.

Place	Date	Hour	Summary of Events and Information	Remarks and references to Appendices
			under Capt J. S. Cawson O.C. and Lieut E. W. Putland	
WELSH CAMP	14-3-18		FORWARD BATTERY H.Qs was situated at MALLARD CROSS ROADS (D5 c.0.5)	
	"		REAR H.Qs at WELSH CAMP. 2 3" Stokes T.M. were placed in VENTURE	
	"		FARM (V.30 A.7.2) and 2 guns at PASSCHENDAELE D.6.13.3.2. These	
	"		guns and teams were under the command of 2/Lt. R. Mulloy	
	"		2 guns were mounted at MEETCHEELE (D.5.13.21) also 2 guns in	
	"		reserve at MALLARD CROSS ROADS D.5 c.0.5. (The latter were in	
	"		position for Anti Aircraft work). The emplacements taken over	
	"		were in very bad condition which entailed a lot of work	
	"		to rebuild same before we could get satisfactory emplacements	
	"		Relief was completed by midnight. Casualties Nil.	
BATTERY H.Q IN THE LINE	15-3-18		Battery on duty in line. Vicinity of MALLARD CROSS ROADS shelled during	
			the day. REAR BATTERY H.Qs (WELSH CAMP) heavily shelled. Railway	
			sidings in vicinity (MANORS JUNCTION) badly damaged. Weather	
			fine. Visibility poor owing to mist. Casualties Nil	
	16-3-18		Battery in line. FWD H.Qs again shelled. (Shrapnel H.E. and "Gas".	
	17-3-18		Battery in line. Weather Very Wet. Enemy shelling Forward and Back	

MAP SHEET C 2 $\frac{1}{10000}$

D. D. & L., London, E.C. (A7883) Wt W809/M1672 350,000 4/17 Sch 52a Forms/C/2118/14

Instructions regarding War Diaries and Intelligence Summaries are contained in F. S. Regs., Part II, and the Staff Manual respectively. Title pages will be prepared in manuscript.

WAR DIARY
or
~~INTELLIGENCE SUMMARY.~~
(Erase heading not required.)

Army Form C. 2118.

Place	Date	Hour	Summary of Events and Information	Remarks and references to Appendices
IN THE LINE	17-3-18		areas. Enemy shelled vicinity of BELLE VUE with "Gas Shells".	
"	18-3-18		Battery in line. Enemy T. Ms active. Our T. M. retaliated on enemy front line. Weather dull.	
"	19-3-18		Battery in line. Heavy shelling forward and back areas all day. Enemy T.M still active. We fired 30 3" Stokes on the Enemy front line in retaliation. S.O.S being sent up our 3" Stokes opened fire on suspected E.T.M Emplacement and Enemy front line. Weather cloudy to fine. 1 O.R from leave to U.K.	
"	20-3-18		Battery in line. Heavy shelling on both sides. Our T M fired 30 rounds on E.T.M Emplacement at EXERT FARM (E.1.A.3.3)	
"	21-3-18		Battery in line. MALLARD CROSS ROADS and vicinity heavily shelled during the day. E.T.M Quiet during day but commenced activity by night. Our 3" Stokes T.M fired 25 shells on TEALL COTT (V.30.B.1.5) Weather Fine but Misty	
"	22-3-18		Battery in Line. Vicinity of Bde H. Qs (FORWARD) heavily shelled for 3 hours. "Gas" shells were fired at MALLARD CROSS ROADS	

MAP SHEET C2 $\frac{1}{10000}$

D. D. & L., London, E.C.
(A7883) Wt W879/M1672 350,000 4/17 Sch 52a Forms/C/2118/14

Army Form C. 2118.

WAR DIARY
or
~~INTELLIGENCE SUMMARY.~~

(Erase heading not required.)

Instructions regarding War Diaries and Intelligence Summaries are contained in F. S. Regs., Part II, and the Staff Manual respectively. Title pages will be prepared in manuscript.

Place	Date	Hour	Summary of Events and Information	Remarks and references to Appendices
IN THE LINE	22-3-18		The gun Teams in front line were relieved by reserve Teams from MALLARD CROSS ROADS and MEETCHEELE. 2/LT A E SMITH relieved 2/LT A MULLOY. Relief completed at 22.00.	
"	23-3-18		Battery in line. Heavy shelling by enemy on our SUPPORT area. PASSCHENDAELE shelled. E.T.M active. They fired 6 or 7 shells. We replied by firing 10 3" Stokes to each 1 fired by enemy. E.T.M were effectively silenced by this method. Hostile aircraft were active during the morning. Weather Fair.	
	24-3-18		Battery in line. Two O.R wounded by M.G fire. Weather fine. Heavy shelling on both sides during day. E.T.M active during night. We replied by firing 70 Rounds 3" Stokes on various targets. Vicinity of BELLE VUE shelled with "gas".	
	25-3-18		Battery in line. Weather cloudy and cold. Very little Artillery activity during day. Activity on both sides by night. E.A flew over our lines very low and fired number of rounds on Duckboard Track and Trenches in vicinity of BELLE VUE	

MAP SHEET C2 $\frac{1}{10000}$

D. D. & L., London, E.C.
(A7883) Wt W809/M1672 350,000 4/17 Sch 52a Forms/C/2118/14

Instructions regarding War Diaries and Intelligence Summaries are contained in F. S. Regs., Part II, and the Staff Manual respectively. Title pages will be prepared in manuscript.

WAR DIARY
or
~~INTELLIGENCE SUMMARY.~~
(Erase heading not required.)

Army Form C. 2118.

Place	Date	Hour	Summary of Events and Information	Remarks and references to Appendices
IN THE LINE	26-3-18		Battery in line. Heavy shelling in vicinity of BELLE VUE. MALLARD CROSS ROADS. and MEETCHEELE during the morning. Very quiet in the afternoon. Our 3" Stokes fired 72 rounds on EXERT FARM and EXERT COPSE. E.T.M were silenced. 40 3" Stokes were fired on the E.M.G emplacements at TEALL COTT. Large number of Gas shells were fired on BELLE VUE during the night. Weather fine. Rear BATTERY H.Q. again shelled.	
"	27-3-18		Battery in line. Vicinity of MEETCHEELE shelled during the day. Otherwise fairly quiet. During the night E.T.M were active at EXERT FARM. At 4.00 the enemy opened fire with heavy bombardment on his S.O.S. lines which lasted about 30 minutes. In reply to this shelling our 3" Stokes fired 90 rounds on TEALL COTT and 80 on EXERT FARM and vicinity. Weather dull and cloudy.	
"	28-3-18		Battery in line. Very quiet during day. Weather Bad. Rain, cloudy. V. Cold. E.T.M fired several shells on the S.O.S.	

MAP SHEET C 2 $\frac{1}{10000}$

D. D. & L., London, E.C.
(A7853) Wt W809/M1672 350,000 4/17 Sch 52a Forms/C/2118/14

Instructions regarding War Diaries and Intelligence Summaries are contained in F. S. Regs., Part II. and the Staff Manual respectively. Title pages will be prepared in manuscript.

WAR DIARY
or
INTELLIGENCE SUMMARY.
(Erase heading not required.)

Army Form C. 2118.

Place	Date	Hour	Summary of Events and Information	Remarks and references to Appendices
IN THE LINE	28-3-18		lines (apparently registering). Our 3" Stokes T.M retaliated with 90 shells on enemy front system. Effectually silencing his T M. Our Aircraft very busy during the morning. Rd Bde order 215	
"	29-3-18		Battery in Line. BELLE VUE and WATERLOO shelled. H E and Gas shells being used. Weather unsettled. Enemy Aircraft active. Received Bde Order 216. TEALL COTT and EXERT FARM were shelled by our 3" Stokes. 20 Rounds were fired on each place. This effectively silenced the E. T. M	
"	30-3-18		Battery in Line. Rear H. Qs (WELSH CAMP) moved to BRAKE CAMP. Heavy shelling in BELLE VUE AREA during day. Battery was relieved by 87th T. M B. Relief under the command of Capt JENNISON arrived at FWD BATTERY H. Qs at 21. 20. All stores maps and defence schemes handed over and receipts obtained. Relief was reported complete to Bde H Qs at 23. 40. The Battery proceeded to SPREE FARM SIDINGS to entrain for BRANDHOEK. While	

MAP SHEET C2 $\frac{1}{10000}$

D. D. & L., London, E.C.
(A7853) Wt W809/M1672 350,000 4/17 Sch 52a Forms/C/2118/14

Instructions regarding War Diaries and Intelligence Summaries are contained in F. S. Regs., Part II, and the Staff Manual respectively. Title pages will be prepared in manuscript.

WAR DIARY
or
~~INTELLIGENCE SUMMARY.~~
(Erase heading not required.)

Army Form C. 2118.

Place	Date	Hour	Summary of Events and Information	Remarks and references to Appendices
IN THE LINE	30-5-16		waiting for the train to leave. The sidings and vicinity	
			of SPREE FARM was heavily shelled. 1 O.R was wounded	
			Arrived at BRANDHOEK at 4 AM and was accomodated in	
			BRAKE CAMP. ~~[illegible]~~	
	31-5-16		Battery Rest. Weather dull and cloudy	

J. S. Lawson Capt
O.C. 86th T.M.B.

D. D. & L., London, E.C.
(A7883) Wt W809/M1672 350,000 4/17 Sch 52a Forms/C/2118/14

MAP SHEET C2 $\frac{1}{10000}$

SECRET.

Copy No. 9

86th Infantry Brigade Order No. 208.

1. The 29th Division (Less Artillery) will relieve the 8th Division (less Artillery) in the left Sector of the VIII Corps Front between the 5th and 8th of March.

2. 86th Infantry Brigade will move to BRANDHOEK AREA on March 7th.
Personnel will move by train and transport by road. - Further details will be issued later by the Staff Captain.

3. On arrival in the 8th Division Area, all troops of the 29th Division will be under orders of the G.O.C., 8th Division until 10 a.m. 8th March when G.O.C. 29th Division will assume command of the Left Sector of VIII Corps Front.

4. All anti-aircraft positions with mountings and sights will be taken over on arrival in BRANDHOEK AREA

5. Completion of move to be reported to Brigade Headquarters at BRAKE CAMP.

6. ACKNOWLEDGE.

Cecil Howard.
Captain,
Brigade Major,
86th Infantry Brigade.

Issued at 4.00 pm.

Copies to :- 1-5 Staff.
6 2/Royal Fusiliers.
7 1/Lancashire Fusiliers.
8 1/Royal Guernsey L.I.
9 86/Trench Mortar Bty.
10 89/Field Ambulance.
11 No. 2 Coy. Div. Train.
12 R.T.O. Caestre.
13 Area Commandant, STEENVOORDE.
14 Sub-Area Commandant, EECKE.
15 Area Commandant, Vlamertinghe.
16 Diary.
17 File.

Unit	FROM	TO	IN RELIEF OF	REMARKS
2/Royal Fusiliers. (2 Coys.)	HASLAR CAMP	Firing Line. (Left) (~~V.30.d.45.40. to V.30.d.50.90.~~)	2/Hampshire Regt. (2Coys.)	
1 Coy.Roy.Fus.	HASLAR CAMP	HOSSELMARKT	1 Coy. 2/Hants.	
1 Coy.Roy.Fus.	HASLAR CAMP	BELLEVUE	1 Coy. 2/Hants.	
1/Lancs.Fusiliers. (2 Coys)	JUNCTION CAMP	Firing Line (right) (~~V.30.d.50.90. to D.6.d.80.90.~~)	1/R.N.F.L.D. Regt. (2 Coys)	
1 Coy.Lancs,Fus.	JUNCTION CAMP.	HOSSELMARKT	1 Coy. R.N.F.L.D.Regt.	
1 Coy.Lancs.Fus.	JUNCTION CAMP.	BELLEVUE	1 Coy. R.N.F.L.D.Regt.	
86th T.M.Battery.	WELSH CAMP.		88th T.M.Battery.	
1/R.G.L.I.	IRISH FARM CAMP	CALIFORNIA CAMP (Brigade Reserve)	4th Worcs.Regt.	

For Brigade and Inter-Battalion Boundaries, see attached map.

2

S E C R E T.
ME
2/Royal Fusiliers.
1/Lancs.Fusiliers.
1/Royal Guernsey L.I.
86th.T.M.B.

14th.March.1918.

ADDENDUM TO 86thINFANTRY BRIGADE ORDER No.209.

1. The 19th Inf.Brigade and the 87th Inf.Brigade have consented to the Right and Left Battalions making use of CRUST FARM and No.6 Tracks respectively.
Units must not cross the GRAVENSTAFEL RIDGE by daylight in parties larger than sections at 200 yards distance.

[signature]
Captain.
for Brigade Major.
86th.Infantry Brigade.

86TMB

Copy No 7

SECRET

13th March 1918.

86th Infantry Brigade Order No.209

1. The 86th Infantry Brigade will relieve the 88th Infantry Brigade in the right sector on the night of the 14/15th March 1918. The command will pass from the G.O.C. 88th Infantry Brigade to the G.O.C.86th Infantry Brigade on completion of relief.

2. Relief will take place in accordance with the attached relief table. All details of relief will be arranged between Units concerned.

3. Units will take over all Defence Schemes, Details of Work in progress and proposed, and Trench stores. Copies of receipts given will be forwarded to these Headquarters.

4. Completion of Relief will be reported in B.A.B. Code to these Brigade Headquarters, which will be established at WATERLOO.

5. ACKNOWLEDGE.

G. Paddison

Captain,
Brigade Major,
86th Infantry Brigade,

Issued at............

Copies to :- 1-3 Staff.
4 2/Royal Fusiliers.
5 1/Lancs.Fusiliers.
6 1/R.Guernsey L.I.
7 86th T.M.Battery.
8 29th Division "G".
9 88th Brigade.
10 87th Brigade.
11 19th Brigade.
12 Diary.
13 File.

SECRET. Copy No.......... 6.

86th INFANTRY BRIGADE ORDER No.210.

Reference map C.2. 1/10000. 16th March 1918.

1. On the night of the 17/18th March, the 1/R.G.L.I. will move from CALIFORNIA CAMP and relieve the 1/Lancs.Fusiliers in the right Battalion sector.

2. After relief the 1/Lancs.Fusiliers will move back to CALIFORNIA CAMP.

3. All details of relief will be arranged between Battalions concerned.

4. All trench stores, Work done and proposed, will be taken over on relief and receipts forwarded to these Headquarters.

5. No work will be done by the Battalion in reserve on the days preceding and following relief.

6. 1/Lancs.Fusiliers will perform two hours work and all their carrying parties before relief.

7. A C K N O W L E D G E.

Issued at.............

P. Cuddon

Captain,
Brigade Major,
86th Inf.Brigade.

Copies to:- 1-2 Staff.
3 2/Royal Fusiliers.
4 1/Lancs.Fusiliers.
5 1/R.Guernsey L.I.
✓6 86th T.M.Battery.
7 87th Inf.Brigade.
8 98th Inf.Brigade.
9 Diary.

4

S E C R E T.

Copy No. 6

86th INFANTRY BRIGADE ORDER No. 211

Reference map C.2. 1/10,000.

March 19th 1918.

1. On the night of the 20-21st March the 1/Lancashire Fusiliers will move from CALIFORNIA CAMP and relieve the 2/Royal Fusiliers in the Left Battalion sector.

2. After relief the 2/Royal Fusiliers will move back to CALIFORNIA CAMP.

3. All details of relief will be arranged between Battalions concerned.

4. All trench stores, work done and proposed, will be taken over on relief and receipts forwarded to these Headquarters.

5. No work will be done by the Battalion in reserve on the days preceding and following relief.

6. The 2/Royal Fusiliers will perform two hours work and all their carrying parties before relief.

7. A C K N O W L E D G E.

Issued at....1630....

R. Cuddon

Captain,
Brigade Major,
86th Inf.Brigade.

Copies to:- 1-2 Staff.
3 2/Royal Fusiliers.
4 1/Lancs.Fusiliers.
5 1/R.Guernsey L.I.
6 86th T.M.Battery.
7 87th Inf.Brigade.
8 98th Inf.Brigade.
9 Diary.

5

SECRET.

Copy No. 6

86TH INFANTRY BRIGADE ORDER NO. 212.

Ref. Map C.2. 1/10000. March 23rd, 1918.

1. On the night of the 24th/25th March, 1918, the 2nd Royal Fusiliers will move from CALIFORNIA CAMP and relieve the 1st Royal Guernsey L.I. in the Right Battalion Sector.

2. After relief the 1st Royal Guernsey L.I. will move back to CALIFORNIA CAMP.

3. All details of relief will be arranged between Battalions concerned.

4. All trench stores, work done and proposed, will be taken over on relief and receipts forwarded to these Headquarters.

5. The 1st Royal Guernsey L.I. will perform two hours work and all their carrying parties before relief.

6. A C K N O W L E D G E.

P. Cadden

Captain,
A/Brigade Major,
86th Infantry Brigade.

Issued at 12 noon

Copies to :- 1-2 Staff.
3 2/Royal Fusiliers.
4 1/Lancashire Fusiliers.
5 1/Royal Guernsey L.I.
6 86/Trench Mortar Bty.
7 88th Infantry Brigade.
8 19th Infantry Brigade.
9 Diary.

6

SECRET.   Copy No. 6

86th. INFANTRY BRIGADE ORDER No.215.

Reference map C.2.   1/10,000.

March 26th.1918.

1. On the night of the 27/28th March the 1/Royal Guernsey L.I. will move from CALAFORNIA CAMP and relieve the 1/Lancs.Fusiliers in the Left Battalion Sector.

2. After relief 3 Companies of the 1/Lancs.Fusiliers will move back to CALAFORNIA CAMP. The remaining Company will move back to the WATERLOO-KRONPRINZ Line and will be accomodated in posts Nos. 7.10.11 and 15.

3. All details of relief will be arranged between Battalions concerned.

4. All trench stores,work done and proposed will be taken over on relief and receipts forwarded to these Headquarters.

5. Relief complete will be reported to these Headquarters in BAB code.

6. The 1/Lancs.Fusiliers will perform two hours work and all their carrying parties before relief.

7. A C K N O W L E D G E.

Issued at 2100...............

Captain.
Brigade Major.
86th.Infantry Brigade.

Copies to:- 1-2 Staff.
3 2/Royal Fusiliers.
4 1/Lancs.Fusiliers.
5 1/Royal Guernsey Light Infantry.
6 86th.T.M.Battery.
7 88th.Infantry Brigade.
8 19th.Infantry Brigade.
9 Diary.

SECRET

SECRET. Copy No.....5....

86th INFANTRY BRIGADE ORDER No. 214

Reference map - 2. 1/10,000.

1. On the night March 27/28th the 86th Infantry Brigade will extend its right to D.6.d.80.35.

2. The 2/Royal Fusiliers will take over from the 1st Camerons Posts Nos. 5,6,7,8, and 8a, and support post called "THE HUT" and PASSCHENDAELE CHURCH.

3. Relief will be carried out as arranged this morning between Brigades and Battalion Commanders concerned.

4. There are two posts 28A and 29A at D.6.d.0.7. and D.6.d.4.9., the first in course of construction by Tunnellers and work has been stopped on the latter. Neither are yet occupied.

5. New Brigade boundary, if any, will be notified later.

6. Completion of relief will be reported to these Headquarters, in B.A.B. Code.

7. ACKNOWLEDGE.

Issued at.....1600.....

Captain,
A/Brigade Major,
86th Infantry Brigade.

Copies to:-
1 - 2 Staff.
3 2/Royal Fusiliers.
4 1/Lancs.Fusiliers.
5 1/R.Guernsey L.I.
6 86th T.M.Battery.
7 88th Inf.Brigade.
8 19th Inf.Brigade.
9 Diary.

S E C R E T.

Copy No. 6

86th INFANTRY BRIGADE ORDER No. 215.

Reference map - C.2. 1/10,000. March 28th 1918.

1. On the night of the 29/30th March the 88th Infantry Brigade will extend their right to the point V.29.b.1.5. road exclusive, taking over posts between that point and the present Inter-Brigade boundary from the 86th Infantry Brigade.

2. The 1st Royal Newfoundland Regt. will take over Posts Nos 15 to 22 from the 1/R.G.L.I. The 1/R.G.L.I. will be responsible for the road.

3. Details of relief will be arranged between Battalion Commanders concerned. (Battalion H.Q. 1/R.Newfoundland Regt. MUIR LODGE).

4. After handing over these posts the 1/R.G.L.I. will extend their right to the point R.1.a.10.85., road inclusive, taking over from the 2/Royal Fusiliers Posts Nos. 10 and 11.

5. Details of relief will be arranged between Battalion Commanders concerned.

6. Completion of relief will be reported to these Headquarters.

7. A C K N O W L E D G E.

Issued at 1800

Captain,
A/Brigade Major,
86th Inf.Brigade.

Copies to:-
1 - 2 Staff.
3 2/Royal Fusiliers.
4 1/Lancs.Fusiliers.
5 1/R.Guernsey L.I.
6 86th T.M.Battery.
7 88th Infantry Brigade.
8 87th Infantry Brigade.
9 29th Division "G".(for information)

9

S E C R E T.

Copy No. 6

86th INFANTRY BRIGADE ORDER No. 216.

Reference maps - Sheets 20 and 28, 1/40,000.
C.2. 1/10,000.

29th March 1918.

1. On the night of the 30/31st March 1918 the 86th Infantry Brigade will be relieved by the 87th Infantry Brigade in the Right Sector of the Divisional Front in accordance with attached relief table.

2. All details of relief will be arranged direct between Officers Commanding Units concerned.

3. Command will pass to the G.O.C. 87th Infantry Brigade at 10 a.m on 31st instant.

4. All copies of 86th Infantry Brigade Defence Scheme, maps, air photos, policy of work and arrangements for work will be handed over on relief. Lists of trench stores handed over will br forwarded to Brigade Headquarters byv April 1st.

5. After relief the 86th Infantry Brigade will move to Divisional Reserve in the BRANDHOEK Area. The necessary train arrangements will be notified by the Staff Captain.

6. Completion of relief will be reported to Brigade Headquarters.

7. After relief Brigade Headquarters will re-open at BRAKE CAMP on arrival.

8. A C K N O W L E D G E.

Issued at 1600

P. Caddon
Captain,
A/Brigade Major,
86th Inf. Brigade.

Copies to:-
1 - 2 Staff
3 2/Royal Fusiliers.
4 1/Lancs.Fusiliers.
5 1/R.Guernsey L.I.
6 86th T.M.Battery.
7 87th Inf.Brigade.
8 88th Inf.Brigade.
9 98th Inf.Brigade.
10 29th Division "G".
11 Diary.

Relief Table issued with 86th Infantry Brigade Order No. 216 dated 29th March [illegible].

Date.	Unit.	From	To	Relieved by	Remarks
Night March 30/31	2 Coys 2/Roy.Fus.	Firing line, right.	"B" Camp	2 Coys 1/K.O.S.B.	
	1 Coy 2/R.Fus.	HOSSELMARKT	ditto	1 Coy. 1/K.O.S.B.	
	1 Coy 2/R.Fus.	BELLEVUE	ditto	1 Coy. 1/K.O.S.B.	
	2 Coys 1/R.G.L.I.	Firing line Left.	RED ROSE CAMP	2 Coys 1/Border Regt.	
	1 Coy.1/RGLI	HOSSELMARKT	ditto	1 Coy. Border Regt.	
	1 Coy 1/R.G.L.I,	BELLEVUE	ditto	1 Coy. Border Regt.	
Morning March 30	2 platoons 1/Lan.Fus.	WATERLOO-KRONPRINZ Line	WARRINGTON CAMP		
	1 Coy.1/L.Fus.	CALIFORNIA CAMP	ditto	1 Coy. 2/S.W.B.	
	2½ Coys.1/L.Fus.	JUNCTION CAMP	ditto	3 Coys 2/S.W.B.	
Night March 30/31	86th T.M.B.	Firing line	BRAKE CAMP	87th T.M.B.	

86th Brigade.

29th Division.

86th LIGHT TRENCH MORTAR BATTERY

APRIL 1918.

Army Form C. 2118.

Instructions regarding War Diaries and Intelligence Summaries are contained in F. S. Regs., Part II, and the Staff Manual respectively. Title pages will be prepared in manuscript.

WAR DIARY
or
~~INTELLIGENCE~~ SUMMARY.
(*Erase heading not required.*)

Place	Date	Hour	Summary of Events and Information	Remarks and references to Appendices
BRAKECAMP	April 1918 1st		Battery cleaning up after being in line - Baths. Received 86th Brigade	
			Order No 216 re next tour in the line. Enemy areoplane shot down in	attached order I
		11.00	BRAKE CAMP which had been dropping bombs on VLAMERTINGHE	
			1 occupant badly wounded 1 unhurt. Weather fine. 3 O.R Hospital.	
"	2nd		Battery preparing for duty in the line. O'C and Sergt Major went up the	
			line to take over from the 98th T.M. Battery - weather showery - 1.O.R Hospital	
"	3rd		Battery moved into the line, leaving BRAKECAMP at 17.00 hrs for	
			ORRILLA SIDINGS where they entrained. detraining IBERNIA SIDINGS	19.30
			Lieut PUTLAND at Headquarters at DASH CROSSING 4 Guns and teams under	
			2/Lt SMITH CREST FARM. 4 Guns and teams under 2/Lt MULLOY	
			at HILLSIDE.	
			O'C and 9. O.R at rear Headquarters at BRAKE CAMP. Relief Completed	
			at 22.45. 1.O.R Hospital. 1.O.R off strength weather showery.	
In the Line	4th		Vicinity of HAMBURG and SEINE shelled at intervals, weather v. bad	
			much rain visibility poor with much mist.	
"	5th		All correct in line. SEINE Shelled at 17.00 hrs. weather dull & cloudy.	C.W.P.

D. D. & L., London, E.C. (A7883) Wt W809/M1672 350,000 4/17 Sch 52a Forms/C/2118/14

Instructions regarding War Diaries and Intelligence Summaries are contained in F. S. Regs., Part II, and the Staff Manual respectively. Title pages will be prepared in manuscript.

WAR DIARY
or
~~INTELLIGENCE~~ SUMMARY.
(Erase heading not required.)

Army Form C. 2118.

Place	Date	Hour	Summary of Events and Information	Remarks and references to Appendices
IN THE LINE	April 6th		Received 86th Brigade Order No 217. Our artillery very active shelling enemy positions weather fine and sunny.	attached II
	7th	10.40	Guns brought out of line under B.S. Major entrained at BORY FARM arriving at BRAKE CAMP at 12.30 hrs. Remainder relieved by 122nd T.M.B at 20.30. By train to BRANDOEK which was reached by 01.30 on 8th Casualties nil. 1.O.R off strength.	
BRAKE CAMP		8th	All surplus kit etc stored at POPERINGHE preparatory to move. Received 86th Bde Order 218 re move	attached III
"		9th	Brigade order 218 cancelled. Stores and advance parties recalled. Received orders to move to MERVILLE AREA. Embussed at BRANDOEK at 22.30 and debussed at VIEUX BERQUIN at 06.15 10th.	attached IV
NEUF BERQUIN		10th	Reached NEUF BERQUIN by march route at 09-15 hrs. Billeted in village awaiting orders. Lieut PUTLAND and 9.O.R. were left at BRAKE CAMP as 10% with surplus stores whence they moved to St JANSTER BIEZEN.	
"		11th	Received orders at 13.00 hrs to move immediately to Bde Hd Qtrs at LES PURESBECQUES. We left at 18.10 hrs en route for PRADELLES	E.W.P.

D. D. & L., London, E.C.
(A7883) Wt WS9/M672 350,000 4/17 Sch 52a Forms/C/2118/14

Army Form C. 2118.

Instructions regarding War Diaries and Intelligence Summaries are contained in F. S. Regs., Part II, and the Staff Manual respectively. Title pages will be prepared in manuscript.

WAR DIARY
or
~~INTELLIGENCE~~ SUMMARY.

(*Erase heading not required.*)

Place	Date	Hour	Summary of Events and Information	Remarks and references to Appendices
			which was reached at 04.15 on 12th Delayed en route through transport getting fast in mud. weather fair.	
PRADELLES	12th		Left PRADELLES at 16.30 for St SYLVESTRE CAPPEL which we reached at 19.15hrs and were billeted in Barns. weather showery.	
St SYLVESTRE CAPPEL	13th		The 10% rejoined Battery at 09.50 from St JANSTER BIEZEN Lieut. PUTLAND and 8 OR. 1 OR being left at St JANSTER BIEZEN with surplus Kit. Received orders to move to HAZEBROUCK AREA, and were on the line of march when orders were received to return to billets. weather fine	
"	14th		86th Brigade came out of the line. Awaiting orders. weather fine	
"	15th		Received orders to be ready to move at an hours notice	
"	16th		Received orders to prepare for moving at a minutes notice. weather conditions cold and showery.	
"	17th		Awaiting orders. weather still unfavourable.	
"	18th		1 Officer 2/Lt MULLOY off strength: returned to Unit 1st R.G.L.I.	
"	19th		Moved at 18.00 hrs to HAZEBROUCK AREA which was reached at 19.30 hrs. and were billeted in 3 small NISSEN HUTS. To be prepared.	E.W.P.

D. D. & L., London, E.C.
(A7283) Wt W809/M1672 350,000 4/17 Sch 52a Forms/C/2118/14

Instructions regarding War Diaries and Intelligence Summaries are contained in F. S. Regs., Part II. and the Staff Manual respectively. Title pages will be prepared in manuscript.

WAR DIARY
or
INTELLIGENCE SUMMARY.
(Erase heading not required.)

Army Form C. 2118.

Place	Date	Hour	Summary of Events and Information	Remarks and references to Appendices
			to move at half an hours notice by day and an hours notice by night 1.OR. off strength. Weather fair.	
HONDEGHEM	20th		Awaiting orders. Battery on Salvage work and training weather fine	
"	21st		Move from V.10A 8.2 at 18.15 to V.1.D.9.5 which we reached at 19.00 and were billeted in a Barn. Weather fine	
"	22nd		Training 1.O.R off strength	
"	23rd		Battery digging under 2nd Royal Fusiliers, weather dull and misty 1.OR off strength	
"	24th		7.O.R (1st R.G.L.I) to Unit on account of Battalion leaving the Brigade. Battery digging with 2nd Royal Fusiliers. Gas chamber at 17.30 hrs. Weather fine.	
"	25th		Battery digging under 2nd Royal Fusiliers 1.O.R. Hospital - weather fair	
"	26th		Training - Received Brigade Order 218. O.C and Sergt Major went up to take over guns from 4th Guards Brigade Weather fair	
"	27th		Battery moved into the line. Left HONDEGHEM at 10.30 arriving at Headquarters at E.26.B.0.7 at 13.45. (MAP SHEET 36A NE 1:20.000)	E.W.P.

D. D. & L., London, E.C.
(A7283) Wt W809/M1672 350,000 1/17 Sch 52a Forms/C/2118/14

Instructions regarding War Diaries and Intelligence Summaries are contained in F. S. Regs., Part II. and the Staff Manual respectively. Title pages will be prepared in manuscript.

WAR DIARY

or

~~INTELLIGENCE SUMMARY.~~

(Erase heading not required.)

Army Form C. 2118.

Place	Date	Hour	Summary of Events and Information	Remarks and references to Appendices
	27th		Two guns under 2/Lt SMITH went into the line one gun at E 27 D.9.6. one gun at E 28.C.0.5. Heavy enemy shelling in parts of wood - weather fair	
NIEPPE FOREST	28th		O.C. Captn J.S LAWSON evacuated sick (later DIAGNOSIS (GAS SHELL WOUND) Lieut PUTLAND took over command Enemy shelling with H E at E.20.D. at 12.50. Aircraft very active in afternoon - Our Artillery very active about 19.00 hrs and all through night weather fair	
"	29th		Our two Gun positions in line heavily shelled by enemy no damage done, weather fair, visibility good at intervals	
"	30th		Received Brigade order to fire 1120 rounds into BEAULIEU FARM E.28.C.0.6. Another Gun was put in line 3 new positions being dug - Zero hour 23.00 After firing a fire was observed on the farm. Weather conditions fair Aircraft v. active also our Artillery	

E. Putland Lieut
a/OC 86 T.M. Battery.

A7092). Wt. W12839/M1293 750,000. 1/17. D, D & L., Ltd. Forms/C2118/14.

2/R. Fus.
1/L. Fus.
1/R.D.F.
1/R.G.A.
1/89 Fd. Ambulance.
510 Fd. Coy. R.E.
86/T.M. Bty.

The 86th & 87th Bdes will move tonight at 8.30 pm. by bus to [illegible] MORBECQUE Area. Buses will be in POPERINGHE – VLAMERTINGHE Rd. for 86th Bde. [illegible] transport will move by road. Probably march 15 miles. [illegible] 2 days rations in addition to [illegible] rations will be taken, [illegible] on the [illegible].
Further details and orders later.
Acknowledge.

[illegible] Capt.
B.M. 86 Inf Bde.

5.30 pm.
9-4-18

"A" Form.

MESSAGES AND SIGNALS

No. of Message

Prefix .... Code .... m.	Words / Charge	This message is on a/c of:	Recd. at .... m.
Office of Origin and Service Instructions	Sent At .... m.	.... Service.	Date
	To		From
	By	(Signature of "Franking Officer.")	By

TO: 3 Batts. / 86 TM Bty / 510 Fld Coy. / No. 2 Coy. Div Train / 89 Fld Ambulance

* Sender's Number	Day of Month	In reply to Number	AAA
BM 32	9		

Ref. Sheet HAZEBROUCK 5A
the 86th Inf. Bde will
embus on the N.W. and
N.E faces of the triangle
formed by the roads
surrounding figure 8 one
metre West of V in
VLAMERTINGHE aaa Head of
column of busses will be
at Rd Junction between
figs. 7 and 8 facing S.E.
Battalions will form up on
edge of Road in following
order Bde HQ. TM Bty. 2 R Fus
~~1/RGLI 2 R Fus 89 Fld Ambulance~~
on S.E. face the 1/RGLI [illegible]
89 Fd. Ambulance 510 Fld Coy RF.

From

Place

Time

The above may be forwarded as now corrected. (Z)

Censor — Signature of Addressor or person authorised to telegraph in his name.

* This line should be erased if not required.

Printed and supplied by Gale & Polden, Ltd., Aldershot, in blocks of 50, 9d. per block, to fit the "Handy Refill Case."

"A" Form.

MESSAGES AND SIGNALS

No. of Message..........

Prefix..........Code..........m.	Words / Charge	This message is on a/c of:	Recd. at..........m.
Office of Origin and Service Instructions	Sent	..........Service.	Date..........
	At..........m.		From..........
	To..........		
	By..........	(Signature of "Franking Officer.")	By..........

TO

Sender's Number	Day of Month	In reply to Number	AAA
*			

on	the	N.W	face	of
triangle.		aaa	Units	
to	be	formed	up	by
8 pm.				

From 81 Bde

Place

Time

The above may be forwarded as now corrected.

(Z) T.F. D[illegible] Capt.

Censor | Signature of Addressor or person authorised to telegraph in his name.

* This line should be erased if not required.

Printed and supplied by Gale & Polden, Ltd., Aldershot, in blocks of 50, 9d. per block, to fit the "Handy Refill Case."

"A" Form.

Army Form C. 2121.
(In pads of 100.)

MESSAGES AND SIGNALS.

No. of Message............

Prefix............Code............m.	Words.	Charge.	This message is on a/c of:	Recd. at ....m.
Office of Origin and Service Instructions.	Sent			Date ZHF 8 IV.18.
	At..........m.		Service	From........
	To..........			
	By..........		(Signature of "Franking Officer.")	By........

SIGNALS

TO 86 TM Bty

Sender's Number.	Day of Month.	In reply to Number.	AAA
* A 792	8		

a lorry reports Bde HQ
1 pm tomorrow to take
kits &c from your unit
and bde ~~[illegible]~~ to
Proven aaa it must be
loaded expeditiously

From	
Place	86 Bde
Time	

The above may be forwarded as now corrected. (Z) P. Riddom Capt

Censor. Signature of Addressor or person authorised to telegraph in his name.

* This line should be erased if not required.

(3796.) Wt. W 492/M1647. 650,000 Pads. 5/17. H.W.&V.Ld. (E. 1187.)

MESSAGES AND SIGNALS.

No. of Message..............

Prefix.......... Code.......... m. | Words. | Charge.

Office of Origin and Service Instructions.

Sent

At..............m.

To..............

By..............

This message is on a/c of:

Service.

(Signature of "Franking Officer.")

Recd. at .... m.

Date

From

By

ARMY SIGNALS

TO 86 T.M. Bty.

Sender's Number.	Day of Month.	In reply to Number.	AAA
* S.C. 1020	8		

Officer in charge of advance party to report at Bde. H.Q. 9 a.m. tomorrow morning AAA To proceed in ambulance to new area to take over billets AAA Remainder of advance party to report to entraining officer at Proven as detailed in O.O. No. 28. AAA Acknowledge

From

Place 88 Bde.

Time

The above may be forwarded as now corrected. (Z) P. [illegible]

Censor. Signature of Addressor or person authorised to telegraph in his name.

* This line should be erased if not required.

(3796.) Wt. W 492/M1647. 650,000 Pads. 5/17. H. W. & V., Ld. (E. 1187.)

HQ 86 Infty Bde
86 Trench Mortar

86th
TRENCH MORTAR
BATTERY.
No. ....
Date 1.6.18

WAR DIARY

FOR

MAY. 1918.

T M B

Army Form C. 2118.

WAR DIARY
or
~~INTELLIGENCE SUMMARY.~~
(Erase heading not required.)

Instructions regarding War Diaries and Intelligence Summaries are contained in F. S. Regs., Part II. and the Staff Manual respectively. Title pages will be prepared in manuscript.

REF 36A NE 1 : 20000

Place	Date	Hour	Summary of Events and Information	Remarks and references to Appendices
	1.5.18		Battery in line. Battery H.Q. at E.26.B.0.7. 3 guns were mounted in the vicinity of E.27.D.8.3. Weather fair.	
	2.5.18		1 Officer and 1 O.R taken on strength. (LIEUT M.J. HARTERY) 1st R.D.F. 1 Officer (CAPT J.S. LAWSON) 9th CHES REGT off strength. Weather fine & dry	
	3.5.18		Guns in line fired 30 rounds on S.O.S lines. LIEUT M J HARTERY took over command of guns in forward positions. BOIS D. AVAL heavily shelled with gas shells at 20.00 on battalion H.Q. Weather very fine. 1. O.R to Hospital 1. O.R off strength.	
	4.5.18		Received Bde order re T.M. barrage for raid on night 5/6 May. Hostile artillery shelled gun emplacements at E.27.D.8.3. Very little damage was done. Ammunition for raid in readiness. Weather fine & warm.	/
	5.5.18		12 O.R's 6th CONNAUGHT RANGERS taken on strength. Fired 5 rounds on S.O.S lines. Fired in conjunction with artillery during raid made by the 1st LANCS FUSILIERS. Each gun fired 32 rounds. (Eight rounds per minute lifting after each minute). The	

A7092). Wt. W12839/M1293. 750,000. 1/17. D. D & L., Ltd. Forms/C2118/14.

Army Form C. 2118.

WAR DIARY
or
~~INTELLIGENCE SUMMARY.~~
(Erase heading not required.)

Instructions regarding War Diaries and Intelligence Summaries are contained in F. S. Regs., Part II. and the Staff Manual respectively. Title pages will be prepared in manuscript.

REF 36A NE 1-20.000

Place	Date	Hour	Summary of Events and Information	Remarks and references to Appendices
	5-5-18		Target engaged was FARM BEAULIEU. 1 O.R wounded. Weather Wet	
	6-5-18		Quiet after the raid. At 20.00 the gun emplacements were shelled by 77 M. shells. No damage. Casualties Nil. 1 O.R off strength	
	7-5-18		3 guns in line under LIEUT M HARTERY registered on S.O.S lines. A good deal of hostile shelling in vicinity of gun emplacements. Weather showery. Casualties Nil.	
	8-5-18		Right Half Battery relieved by Left Half in line. A heavy barrage was put down on our front line posts by enemy at 12 Midnight 02.00 and 04.00 but no infantry action followed	
	9-5-18		Our artillery active in reply to enemy shelling. 3" S.T.M fired 20 rounds at suspected E.T.M. There was no retaliation. BOIS D AVAL bombed by E. Aircraft about 20 bombs being dropped. 1 O.R to Hospital. Weather dull Misty. Visibility poor.	
	10-5-18		E Aircraft again active. E. artillery active. Also our own. Weather dull making observation difficult.	
	11-5-18		Our forward gun emplacements at E.29 D. were heavily shelled by	WLS

Army Form C. 2118.

Instructions regarding War Diaries and Intelligence Summaries are contained in F. S. Regs., Part II. and the Staff Manual respectively. Title pages will be prepared in manuscript.

WAR DIARY
or
~~INTELLIGENCE SUMMARY.~~
(Erase heading not required.)

REF 36A NE 1:20000

Place	Date	Hour	Summary of Events and Information	Remarks and references to Appendices
	11-5-18		hostile artillery and house set on fire. Several parts of the guns and equipment were lost in the fire. Guns and teams were withdrawn from this position. Casualties Nil. E. Aircraft less active than usual. Weather fair.	
	12-5-18		Received Bde Order re raid on night 13/14. 5 guns to give [illegible] steady fire for 20 minutes in vicinity of FARM BEAULIEU. Emplacements sited and dug. Sheets prepared. Weather fair Visibility good.	II
	13-5-18		Raid postponed. Enemy shelled BOIS D AVAL. Weather good.	
	14-5-18		Raid carried out by 2nd ROYAL FUSILIERS. a S.T.M barrage was put down by the 5 guns. Firing from ZERO to plus 30 486 rounds were fired. Casualties 5 O.R. (3 Wounded) (2 gassed) The enemy put down heavy barrage on our gun positions at E edge of BOIS. D. AVAL. Weather showery Visibility: Poor.	
	15-5-18		LIEUT W. B. SOLLY took command of the Battery. 1 gun withdrawn from the forward positions leaving 2 guns in line. Part of	W.B.S.

Instructions regarding War Diaries and Intelligence Summaries are contained in F. S. Regs., Part II. and the Staff Manual respectively. Title pages will be prepared in manuscript.

WAR DIARY
or
INTELLIGENCE SUMMARY.
(Erase heading not required.)

Army Form C. 2118.

REF 36A NE 1:20000

Place	Date	Hour	Summary of Events and Information	Remarks and references to Appendices
	15-5-18		Battery went out of the line for a rest. Weather fair.	
	16-5-18		E. artillery v active. Baths for men resting at LE TIR ANGLAIS	
	17-5-18		Usual artillery activity. BOIS D AVAL heavily shelled with H.E and gas. Weather warm. Visibility good.	
	18-5-18		Received Bde Order for move No 222 and 223. Weather fine.	III
	19-5-18		Battery relieved by 88th T.M.B. Relief completed by 20.00. Marched to C.12 D.6.6. Accommodated in Bell tents. Move completed by 22.40. Weather good.	
	20-5-18		Battery cleaning up guns, equipment etc. 1 O.R on strength ex Hospital	
	21-5-18		Baths allotted to Battery. Training. Lecture etc. 1 O.R to Hospital	
	22-5-18		Training continued. Gun Drill. Firing. Rapid digging emplacements. 3 O.R returned to Unit (off strength). Weather good.	
	23-5-18		Training continued. LIEUT W. BOWLES assumed command of Battery. 1 O.R to Hospital. Weather wet.	
	24-5-18		Training. Lectures. Drill etc. 2 O.R to Hospital.	
	25-5-18		Training etc. Received Bde Order No 225. Pte Sarling B awarded Military Medal	[illegible]

Instructions regarding War Diaries and Intelligence Summaries are contained in F. S. Regs., Part II. and the Staff Manual respectively. Title pages will be prepared in manuscript.

WAR DIARY
or
INTELLIGENCE SUMMARY.
(Erase heading not required.)

Army Form C. 2118.

REF 36A NE 1:20000

Place	Date	Hour	Summary of Events and Information	Remarks and references to Appendices
	26-5-18		LIEUT. W. BOWLES and LIEUT. E. PUTLAND reconnoitred front line and gun positions. Weather fine. Battery preparing for move.	
	27-5-18		Battery relieved the 87th T.M.B. 2 guns were mounted in front line and one gun in reserve for raids patrols etc. under command of 2/Lt A. SMITH. 2 guns were mounted in support line under the command of LIEUT. M. HARTERY. 3 guns in reserve at Battery H.Q. at D.18.b.67.57. Relief was completed by 12-30 AM.	
	28-5-18		Battery on duty in line. H.Q. heavily shelled at intervals during the day. 1 O.R struck off strength.	
	29-5-18		Battery in line. Enemy Artillery very active. Casualties in line 1 O.R Killed 2 O.R wounded by enemy shell fire. Weather very good.	
	30-5-18		Battery in line. Enemy artillery very active all day. 1 Officer (LIEUT. W. SCULLY) 1 O.R off strength. Weather fine. 1 O.R from Hospital.	WB
	31-5-18		Received Bde Order 226. New emplacements selected for guns in	

Army Form C. 2118.

WAR DIARY
or
INTELLIGENCE SUMMARY.
(Erase heading not required.)

Instructions regarding War Diaries and Intelligence Summaries are contained in F. S. Regs., Part II. and the Staff Manual respectively. Title pages will be prepared in manuscript.

REF 36 A NE 1-20000

Place	Date	Hour	Summary of Events and Information	Remarks and references to Appendices
	31.5.18		Front line. Heavy enemy shelling at night. H.E and Gas being used. 2. O.R from Hospital	

W Bowles Lt.
Cmdg 86 T.M. Bty

A7092). Wt. W12839/M1293 750,000. 1/17. D. D & L., Ltd. Forms/C2118/14.

I.

S E C R E T. 86th Inf.Brigade No. G.92/22

Raid to be carried out by 86th Infantry Brigade

on night of 5th/6th May 1918.

1. **OBJECTIVE.**

The 1/Lancs.Fusiliers will carry out a raid on the night of the 5th/6th May on RUE BEAULIEU from the South, searching all houses, enclosures and hedges in the vicinity, returning by the VERTE RUE Road to E.20.c.1.2.

2. **OBJECT.**

The object of the raid is to obtain prisoners and to kill Germans.

3. **STRENGTH OF RAIDING PARTY.**

The raiding party will consist of 2 Officers and 58 other ranks who will be split up into five parties.

4. **ASSEMBLY.**

The raiding party will be assembled at K.4.b.5.1. at Zero minus five minutes.

5. **ARTILLERY.**

The artillery barrage will be carried out by the 152nd Brigade R.F.A. and 285th Brigade R.F.A. with two batteries of 6" howitzers firing on selected points in rear.

Artillery arrangements are as follows:-

(a) **A/152. Zero to 0 plus 5.**

K.4.b.50.60. to K.4.b.30.60. thence by switches of 1 deg. lift every three minutes to E.28.d.30.40. to E.28.c.90.30. thence to protective barrage till 0 plus 60. E.28.d.30.85. to E.28.c.90.90.

B/152. Zero to 0 plus 5.

K.4.b.75.60. to K.4.b.50.60. thence by switches of 1 deg. lift every three minutes to E.28.d.50.50. to E.28.d.30.40. thence to protective barrage till 0 plus 60. E.28.d.9.9. to E.28.d.30.85.

C/152. Superimpose. Zero to 0 plus 5.

Line E.28.d.1.0. to E.28.d.6.0. thence to protective barrage by switches of 1 deg. lift every three minutes. E.28.c.9.9. to E.28.d.9.9. till 0 plus 60.

(b) 285th Brigade R.F.A. 3 18pdr batteries.
From Zero to 0 plus 3. E.29.b.0.3. - K.5.b.7.7. thence to protective barrage E.28.d.9.9. - K.5.a.5.2. by drops of 100 yds every three minutes and remain till 0 plus 60.

(c) **D/152. and D/285. 4.5 Hows.superimpose. From Zero to 0 plus3.**
E.28.d.7.2. - K.4.b.9.8. thence to protective barrage E.29.a.8.3. - E.29.d.4.5. by lifts of 100 yards every 3 minutes and remain on protective till 0 plus 60.

(d) 1. 6" How. E.23.c.9.8.
1 " " E.29.a.35.95.
1 " " K.5.b.50.75.
1 " " K.5.d.35.50.
2 " " K.11.a.5.5. and vicinity.

(e) 1 " " E.29.c.85.65.)
1 " " E.29.c.8.2.) Zero to plus 20.
then lift to LA COURONNE and vicinity till 0 plus 60.

(f) **Rates of fire.**

18pdrs.	Zero to Protective barrage.	4 rounds	p.g.p.m.
	Protective to 0 plus 50.	2 "	" "
	0 plus 50 to 0 plus 60.	1 "	" "
4.5 Hows.	Half of above rates.		

5 contd. A Brigade of R.F.A. is also being asked for from the Vth Division to fire on hedges in ~~K.5.b.~~ during the operation. K.5.a+c.

6. MACHINE GUNS.

Eight machine guns will fire from positions at E.22.b.0.4. These guns will sweep the hedges in the vicinity of VERTE RUE from E.28.d.9.5. to Road junction at E.29.c.8.6. from Zero to Zero plus 60 minutes.

Machine Guns and Lewis Guns of the Vth Division are also being asked to fire bursts on L'EPINETTE and K.11.a. from Zero until Zero plus 60 minutes.

7. STOKES GUNS.

Seven Stkos guns will fire from positions at E.28.c.30.35. and E.28.c.30.15. from Zero until Zero plus 4 min. on FARM BEAULIEU and hedges in the vicinity. These guns will not fire South of a line K.4.b.2.8. - K.4.b.6.8.

8. ACTION OF RAIDING PARTY.

At Zero the scouts and five parties will move forward getting close up to the barrage ready to assault at Zero plus 5 minutes. The raiding party will follow the barrage at Zero plus 5 minutes, numbers 1 and 2 Parties making holes in the Southern edge of hedges round FARM BEAULIEU at about K.4.b.60.65. and searching all fields and houses south of the VERTE RUE.

Nos 3, 4 and 5 Parties will move along the eastern hedge running from K.4.b.70.65. - E.28.d.40.50. keeping close to the barrage. Nos 3 and 4 Parties will search all ground and houses in the enclosures north of VERTE RUE.

No. 5 Party (Lewis Gun) will halt at about E.28.d.60.15. and act as a covering party to the remainder of the raiding party.

The raiding party will not remain in FARM BEAULIEU later than Zero plus 40 minutes.

9. SIGNALS.

A rocket bursting into gold and silver rain will be the signal for the raiding party to retire.

10. SYNCHRONISATION OF WATCHES.

Watches will be synchronised at 86th Infantry Brigade H.Q. at 5 p.m. May 5th.

11. ZERO HOUR.

Zero hour will be notified later.

12. A C K N O W L E D G E.

J.F. Dearden Captain,
Brigade Major,
86th Inf.Brigade.

Copies to:-
1. 2/Royal Fusiliers.
2. 1/Lancs.Fusiliers.
3. 1/R.Dublin Fusiliers.
4. 86th T.M.Battery. ✓
5. 87th Inf.Brigade.
6. 88th Inf.Brigade.
7. 13th Inf.Brigade.
8. 29th Division 'G'.
9. 29th M.G.Battalion.
10. 152nd Brigade R.F.A.
11. 285th Brigade R.F.A.

SECRET.

86th Inf.Brigade No. G.92/22.

To All recipients
of 86th Inf.
Brigade No. G.92/22
of 4/5/18.

May 5th, 1918

Reference this Office No. G.92/22 dated 4th May 1918.

1. Zero hour will be 2-50 a.m. on the night of 5th/6th May.

2. The 160th Brigade R.F.A. will put down a standing barrage as follows:-

3 - 18 pdr batteries.

Along hedge and ditch K.10.b.70.55. - K.4.d.83.05. -

K.5.c.00.20. - K.5.c.60.55. - K.5.a.50.20.

Rate of fire.

Zero to plus 60 - half round p.g.p.m.

3. ACKNOWLEDGE.

Issued at.............

J.F. Dearden Captain,
Brigade Major,
86th Inf.Brigade.

86th T.M.B.

II

86th Inf.Brigade No. G.92/28.

To All Recipients of
86th Inf.Brigade No.
G.92/28 of 13th May.

1. The 2/Royal Fusiliers will carry out the raid referred to in this Office No. G.92/28 of 13th inst., and cancelled, for the night of the 13/14th May, on the night of the 14/15th May.

2. Artillery, Machine Gun and Stokes barrages will be carried out in accordance with the original plan.

3. Zero hour will be 1 a.m. and not 1-30 a.m. as previously stated.

4. Watches will be synchronised at Brigade H.Q. at 7 pm 14th May.

5. A lorry will be at the huts at E.25.a.6.9. at 4 a.m. May 15th to bring the raiding party back to the Divisional Reserve Battn.

6. ACKNOWLEDGE.

14th May 1918.

J.F. Dearden Captain,
Brigade Major,
86th Inf.Brigade.

111

S E C R E T.

~~To~~ All Recipients
of 86th Inf.Bde
Order No. 223

AMENDMENT to 86th Inf.Brigade Order No. 223.

Reference 86th Bde Order No. 223.

Cancel lines 4 and 5 in para 1.

The Post of the 1/Lancs.Fusiliers at K.4.a.5.2. will be handed over to the 1/D.C.L.I. tonight and will not be taken over by the 1/R.Dublin Fusiliers.

18th May 1918.

J.F. Dearden. Captain,
Brigade Major,
86th Inf.Brigade.

S E C R E T.

Copy No......6

86th INFANTRY BRIGADE ORDER No. 223

Ref. map - 36 A. N.E.
1/20,000.

18th May 1918.

1. On the night of 18/19th May, the 1/Lancs.Fusiliers will hand over to the 1/D.C.L.I. that portion of the Brigade Front between present Southern boundary and K.4.a.6.0.
The Post of the 1/Lancs.Fusiliers at K.4.a.5.2. will be handed over to the Right Coy. of the 1/R.Dublin Fusiliers.
Details of relief will be arranged between Battalion Commanders concerned.

2. S.A.A. and other trench stores will be handed over and receipts obtained for them.

3. Such adjustment of the artillery barrage as may be necessary will be arranged direct between Cs.R.A. 29th and 5th Divisions.

4. On completion of relief, the new southern boundary of 29th Division and 86th Infantry Brigade will be K.4.central-K.3.central, ECLUSE GRAND DAM K.2.a.4.0. then along the centre of the Canal to Canal Junction at D.30.c.8.3., thence along present boundary.

5. Completion of relief will be reported to Brigade Headquarters by the code word "HALT".

6. A C K N O W L E D G E.

Issued at..........

F.F. Dearden
Captain,
Brigade Major,
86th Inf.Brigade.

Copies to:-
1 - 2 Staff.
3 2/Royal Fusiliers.
4 1/Lancs.Fusiliers.
5 1/R.Dublin Fusiliers.
6 86th T.M.Battery.
7 87th Inf.Bde.
8 88th Inf.Bde.
9 95th Inf.Bde.
10 29th Division 'G'.
11 29th Div. Artillery.
12 Bde Signal Officer.
13 29th M.G.Battalion.
14 O.C . Reserve Line.
15 A.D.M.S.
16 Diary.
17 File.

"A" Form.
MESSAGES AND SIGNALS.

Army Form C. 2121.
(In pads of 100.)
No. of Message

Prefix ... Code ... m.	Words. Charge.	This message is on a/c of:	Recd. at ... m.
Office of Origin and Service Instructions.	Sent At ... m. To By	Service. (Signature of "Franking Officer.")	Date From By

TO ~~[illegible]~~ T M Bty.

Sender's Number.	Day of Month.	In reply to Number.	
* C.178	15		AAA

Ref Brigade Order
222 para 4
Nobby

From
Place
Time

Q.U.Q.A.

The above may be forwarded as now corrected. (Z)

Censor. Signature of Addressor or person authorised to telegraph in his name.

* This line, except **AAA**, should be erased if not required.

Wt. W 3253/P511. 500,000 Pads. 1/18. B. & S. Ltd. (E2389.)

G12
30

SECRET.

2/Royal Fusiliers.
1/Lancs.Fusiliers.
1/R.Dublin Fusiliers.
86th T.M.Battery.
O.C. Reserve Line.

86th INFANTRY BRIGADE ORDER No. 222.

1. Projectors have been installed on the Divisional Front at E.22.b.30.25. and E.16.a.70.35. by "L" Special Coy., R.E.

2. These projectors will be fired against the following targets on the night of the 15/16th May or first subsequent night of favourable weather conditions at a Zero hour to be notified later (approximately 2-0 a.m.).

Target.	No. of drums.
E.29.c.5.5.	115
E.29.d.3.8.	160
E.17.d.5.8.	171

3. Wind limits are S.W. by W. to N.N.W. through W.

4. Brigade will notify Units if conditions are favourable or otherwise. The following Code words will be used:-

BON - conditions favourable gas will be discharged.
NOBBY - conditions unfavourable operations postponed 24 hours.

5. The 29th Divisional Artillery will arrange for a burst of covering fire from Zero minus 10 to Zero plus 5 minutes.

6. For the purpose of this operation, all Officers of "L" Special Coy. R.E. will have urgent priority rights over the whole of the Divisional communications.

7. ACKNOWLEDGE.

15th May 1918.

F.F. Dearden Captain,
Brigade Major,
86th Inf.Brigade.

IV

SECRET.

86th INFANTRY BRIGADE ADMINISTRATIVE ORDER No. 27.

Issued with Brigade Order No. 224.

Ref. map - 36 A. 1/40,000. 18th May 1918.

1. BILLETS. On relief, Units will take over billets in the new area as follows:-
   (a) 2/Royal Fusiliers, from the 2/Hampshire Regt.
   Locations are as follows:- H.Q. D.6.d.91.85.
   1 Coy.E.7.b.30.95.
   1 Coy.ODE HARQUETTE FME.
   1 Coy.D.12.a.2.1.
   1 Coy. LE RIEST D.10.c.2.7.

   (b) 1/Lancs.Fusiliers.from the 4/Worc.Regt.
   Camp (Nissen Huts) at LE GRAND HASARD D.14.b.2.4.

   (c) 1/R.Dublin Fusiliers. from the 2/Leinster Regt.
   Camp (Nissen Huts) at LE GRAND HASARD D.14.b.2.4.

   (d) 86th T.M.Battery from 88th T.M.Battery at C.12.d.6.6. (Tents).

2. HEADQUARTERS. Brigade H.Q. will be at D.13.a.1.8. the Rear H.Q. Office will remain at WALLON CAPPEL.

3. TRANSPORT LINES. Transport Lines and Q.M.Stores will remain where they now are.

4. DUTIES. The following patrols will be found:-
   (1) By 1/Lancs.Fusiliers.
   (a) One N.C.O. and 10 men as loading party at R.E. dump at D.2.d.6.6. to relieve the party of the 2/Leinster Regt by 12 noon, 19th inst. This party will be rationed by the R.E.
   (b) One N.C.O. and 10 men to report at 6 p.m. on 19th inst. to O.C. Military Police at MORBECQUE. Accommodation will be provided there but the party will be rationed by its own unit.

   (2) By 1/R.Dublin Fusiliers.
   One Officer and 20 O.R. for patrol duty at HAZEBROUCK under the A.P.M. This party will meet a guide from the present picquet (1/Leinster Regt) at 12 noon at the X Roads (D.14.b.00.05.) on 19th instant. The Offiver incharge will take over all duties from the O.i/c Picket, 1/Leinster Regt.
   The party will be billetted in HAZEBROUCK but will be ratio ed by its own unit.

5. BATHS. At LE GRAND HAZARD,D.14.b.5.8. Arrangements will be notified later.

6. AMMUNITION. Div. Ammunition Dump is at D.8.c.9.9.

7. A C K N O W L E D G E.

C Barrington Brown
Captain,
Staff Captain,
86th Inf.Brigade.

Issued at 9.30am 19/5/18

Copies to:-
1-2 Staff.
3-4 2/Roy.Fus.Rear & Ford.
5-6 1/Lancs.Fus. do do
7-8 1/R.Dub.Fus. do do
9 86th T.M.Battery. ✓
10 86th Bde Rear H.Q.
11 88th Brigade.
12 29th Division 'Q'.
13 B.T.O.
14 Area Comdt MORBECQUES.
15 do do SERCUS.
16 C.R.E. 29th Div.
17 Diary.
18 File.

Instructions regarding War Diaries and Intelligence Summaries are contained in F. S. Regs., Part II. and the Staff Manual respectively. Title pages will be prepared in manuscript.

WAR DIARY
or
INTELLIGENCE SUMMARY.
(Erase heading not required.)

Army Form C. 2118.

REF 36a NE 1 20000

Place	Date	Hour	Summary of Events and Information	Remarks and references to Appendices
	1.5.18		Battery in line. Battery H.Q. at E.26.B.0.7. 3 guns were forward in the vicinity of E.27.D.8.3. Weather fine.	
	2.5.18		1 Officer and 1 O.R. taken on strength (LIEUT M. J. HARTERY) 1st R.D.F. 1 Officer (CAPT J S LAWSON) 9th CHES REGT off strength. Weather fine & dry. Guns in line fired 30 rounds on S.O.S. lines. LIEUT M. J. HARTERY	
	3.5.18		took over command of guns in forward positions. BOIS D AVAL heavily shelled with gas shells at 20.00 no casualties. Weather very fine. 1 O.R. to Hospital. 1 O.R. off strength.	
	4.5.18		Received Bde order re T M barrage for raid on night 5/6 May. Hostile artillery shelled gun emplacements at E.27.D.8.3. Very little damage was done. Ammunition for raid in readiness. Weather fine & warm.	
	5.5.18		12 O.R. 6th CONNAUGHT RANGERS taken on strength. Fired 5 rounds on S.O.S. lines. Fired in conjunction with artillery during raid made by the 1st LANCS FUSILIERS. Each gun fired 32 rounds (Eight rounds per minute lifting after each minute). The	

A7092). Wt. W12839/M1293. 750,000. 1/17. D. D & L., Ltd. Forms/C2118/14.

Instructions regarding War Diaries and Intelligence Summaries are contained in F. S. Regs., Part II. and the Staff Manual respectively. Title pages will be prepared in manuscript.

WAR DIARY
or
INTELLIGENCE SUMMARY.
(Erase heading not required.)

Army Form C. 2118.

REF 36A NE 1-20000

Place	Date	Hour	Summary of Events and Information	Remarks and references to Appendices
	5-5-18		Target engaged was FARM BEAULIEU. 1 O.R. wounded. Weather W[illegible]	
	6-5-18		Quiet after the raid. At 20.00 the gun emplacements were shelled by 77 m/m shells. No damage. Casualties nil. 1 O.R. off strength.	
	7-5-18		3 guns in line under LIEUT M HARTERY registered on S.O.S lines. A good deal of hostile shelling in vicinity of gun emplacements. Weather showery. Casualties nil.	
	8-5-18		Right Half Battery relieved by Left Half in line. A heavy barrage was put down on our front line posts by enemy at 12 midnight, 01.00 and 04.00 but no infantry action followed.	
	9-5-18		Our artillery active in reply to enemy shelling. 3" S.T.M fired 20 rounds at suspected E.T.M. There was no retaliation. BOIS D'AVAL bombed by E. Aircraft about 20 bombs being dropped. 1 O.R. to Hospital. Weather dull misty. Visibility poor.	
	10-5-18		E. Aircraft again active. E. Artillery active. Also our own. Weather dull making observation difficult.	
	11-5-18		Our forward gun emplacements at E.29.D were heavily shelled by	[illegible]

A7092). Wt. W12839/M1293 750,000. 1/17. D. D & L., Ltd. Forms/C2118/14.

Instructions regarding War Diaries and Intelligence Summaries are contained in F. S. Regs., Part II. and the Staff Manual respectively. Title pages will be prepared in manuscript.

WAR DIARY
or
INTELLIGENCE SUMMARY.
(Erase heading not required.)

Army Form C. 2118.

REF 36A NE 1:20000

Place	Date	Hour	Summary of Events and Information	Remarks and references to Appendices
	11-5-18		hostile artillery and house set on fire. Several parts of the guns and equipment were lost in the fire. Guns and teams were withdrawn from this position. Casualties nil. E. Aircraft less active than usual. Weather fair.	
	12-5-18		Received Bde Orders re raid on night 13/14. 5 guns to give [illegible] steady fire for 20 minutes in vicinity of FARM BEAULIEU. Emplacements sited and dug. Shells prepared. Weather fair. Visibility good.	
	13-5-18		Raid postponed. Enemy shelled BOIS D AVAL. Weather good.	
	14-5-18		Raid carried out by 2nd ROYAL FUSILIERS. a S.T.M barrage was put down by the 5 guns. Firing from ZERO to plus 30. 496 rounds were fired. Casualties 5 O.R. (3 Wounded) (2 Gassed). The enemy put down heavy barrage on our gun positions at E edge of BOIS. D. AVAL. Weather showery. Visibility. Poor.	
	15-5-18		LIEUT W. B. SOLLY took command of the Battery. 1 gun withdrawn from the forward positions leaving 2 guns in line. Part of	W.S.

A7092). Wt. W12839/M1293 750,000. 1/17. D. D & L., Ltd. Forms/C2118/14.

Instructions regarding War Diaries and Intelligence Summaries are contained in F. S. Regs., Part II. and the Staff Manual respectively. Title pages will be prepared in manuscript.

Army Form C. 2118.

WAR DIARY
or
INTELLIGENCE SUMMARY.
(Erase heading not required.)

REF 36A NE 1:20000

Place	Date	Hour	Summary of Events and Information	Remarks and references to Appendices
	15-5-18		Battery went out of the line for a rest. Weather fine.	
	16-5-18		E battery V active. B area for men resting at LE TIR ANGLAIS	
	17-5-18		Usual artillery activity. BOIS D'AVAL heavily shelled with H.E. and gas. Weather warm. Visibility good	
	18-5-18		Received Bde Orders for move to 222 and 223. Weather fine.	
	19-5-18		Battery relieved by 92nd T.M.B. Relief completed by 20.00. Marched to L.12.D.6.6. Accommodation in Bde Area. Move completed by 23.40. Weather good	
	20-5-18		Battery cleaning up guns equipment etc. 1 O.R. on strength Hospital	
	21-5-18		Baths allotted to Battery. Training carried out. 1 O.R. to Hospital	
	22-5-18		Training continued. Gun Drill. Firing. Rapid digging emplacements. 3 O.R. returned to unit (off strength). Weather good.	
	23-5-18		Training continued. Lieut W. BOWLES assumed command of Battery. 1 O.R. to Hospital. Weather wet.	
	24-5-18		Training carried out. Drill etc. 2 O.R. to Hospital.	
	25-5-18		Training etc. [illegible] Bde T.M. 225. Pte [illegible] B awarded Military Medal	

A7092). Wt. W12639/M1293 750,000. 1/17. D. D & L., Ltd. Forms/C2118/14.

Army Form C. 2118.

WAR DIARY
or
INTELLIGENCE SUMMARY.
(Erase heading not required.)

Instructions regarding War Diaries and Intelligence Summaries are contained in F. S. Regs., Part II. and the Staff Manual respectively. Title pages will be prepared in manuscript.

Ref. 36A NE 1:20000

Place	Date	Hour	Summary of Events and Information	Remarks and references to Appendices
	26-5-18		LIEUT W BOWLES and LIEUT G. PUTLAND reconnoitred front line and gun positions. Weather fine. Battery preparing for move.	
	27-5-18		Battery relieved the 27th T.M.B. 2 guns were mounted in front line and one gun in reserve for raids patrols etc. Under command of 2/LT A SMITH. 2 guns were mounted in support line under the command of LIEUT M. HARTERY. 3 guns in reserve at Battery H.Qs at D.18.B.67.27. Relief was completed by 11.30 A.M.	
	28-5-18		Battery on duty in line. H.Q. heavily shelled at intervals during the day. 1 O.R struck off strength.	
	29-5-18		Battery in line. Enemy artillery very active. Casualties in line 1 O.R killed 2 O.R wounded by enemy shell fire. Weather very good.	
	30-5-18		Battery in line. Enemy artillery very active all day. 1 Officer (LIEUT W. SOLLY) 1 O.R off strength. Weather fine. 1 O.R from Hospital.	
	31-5-18		Received Bde Order 226. New emplacements selected for guns in	

A7092). Wt. W12839/M1293 750,000. 1/17. D. D & L., Ltd. Forms/C2118/14.

Army Form C. 2118.

WAR DIARY
or
INTELLIGENCE SUMMARY.
(Erase heading not required.)

Instructions regarding War Diaries and Intelligence Summaries are contained in F. S. Regs., Part II. and the Staff Manual respectively. Title pages will be prepared in manuscript.

REF 36A NE 1:20000

Place	Date	Hour	Summary of Events and Information	Remarks and references to Appendices
	31-5-18		Front line. Heavy enemy shelling at night H.E. and Gas being used. 2. O.R from Hospital	

C. Bowles Lt
Cmdg 56 T M Bty

A7092). Wt. W12839/M1293 750,000. 1/17. D. D & L., Ltd. Forms/C2118/14.

Instructions regarding War Diaries and Intelligence Summaries are contained in F. S. Regs., Part II. and the Staff Manual respectively. Title pages will be prepared in manuscript.

WAR DIARY
or
~~INTELLIGENCE SUMMARY.~~
(Erase heading not required.)

Army Form C. 2118.

REF. MAP. 36A NE.

Place	Date	Hour	Summary of Events and Information	Remarks and references to Appendices
	June 1st		Battery in Line. Orders from Brigade that minor operations arranged for 1/2nd June postponed for 24 hrs. (Bde order 227 att:) Enemy artillery very quiet.	I
			Brigade order 228 received.	II
	2nd		Fired 480 rounds in co-operation with the Artillery, when a barrage was put down to cover the 2nd Royal Fusiliers, and 1st Dublin Fusiliers when they attacked the Enemy's positions in E.17 – E.23 (Sheet 36 NE (Ed 7)). We had Eight guns in the line supported by two guns and teams lent by the 87th T.M. Battery. Two guns went forward with the advance, 1 gun and team with the 2nd Royal Fusiliers, and one gun & team with the 1st Royal Dublin Fusiliers. Casualties – 2. O.R. Killed, 2. O.R. wounded.	
	3rd	23.45	Enemy put down Barrage in support of a bombing raid on our new positions. Our Artillery replied and enemy was repulsed. Our T.M's fired 20 rounds. Casualties 5. O.R. wounded. Bde Order 229 (received)	III
	4th		Fired on suspected M.G. emplacement (6 rounds) Neighbourhood of Bty Hd Q, vis D.18.A & B shelled with Gas. Weather very fine.	
	5th		Our gun positions badly shelled by 5.9s and Gas. No damage was done however. 1. O.R. accidentally wounded by Stokes detonator.	[initials]

A7092). Wt. W12839/M1293 750,000. 1/17. D. D & L., Ltd. Forms/C2118/14.

Instructions regarding War Diaries and Intelligence Summaries are contained in F. S. Regs., Part II. and the Staff Manual respectively. Title pages will be prepared in manuscript.

WAR DIARY
or
~~INTELLIGENCE SUMMARY~~.
(Erase heading not required.)

Army Form C. 2118.

REF MAP 36A NE.

Place	Date	Hour	Summary of Events and Information	Remarks and references to Appendices
	6th		Quiet day in line. 1 OR Hospital	
	7th		Nothing to report. Weather still very fine	
	8th		Quiet in line. O.C. Captain W Bowles left for 14 days leave to U.K. Lieut E.W. PUTLAND. took over Command. Brigade order 231 received.	IV
	9th		All quiet in line - 1. O.R Hospital Weather stormy.	
	10th		Fired 42 rounds on suspected M.G. position about E 23. c 85 at 02.00 Ref map 36A NE (Ed 7) 12 OR on strength.	
	11th		Received Brigade order 232 re Gas attack (order handed over to 88 T.M.B on relief) Brigade order 233 received re relief on night of the 12th/13th	X
			Quiet day very little enemy shelling. weather fine. Orders to evacuate to support line in connection with Gas attack Guns and teams were withdrawn at 23.00 hrs. Wind proved unfavourable and line was re-occupied at 02.30.	
	12th		On night of 12th/13th Battery was relieved by 88th T.M. Battery, 4 guns being handed over by either side. Relief completed by 00.10. 13.6.18. Battery was accomodated in Camp at C.12.D.5.6. (Map 36A N.E.) in tents which was reached at 02.15.	
	13.		Battery resting and cleaning up. weather fine -	WB

A7092). Wt. W12839/M1293 750,000. 1/17. D. D & L., Ltd. Forms/C2118/14.

Instructions regarding War Diaries and Intelligence Summaries are contained in F. S. Regs., Part II. and the Staff Manual respectively. Title pages will be prepared in manuscript.

WAR DIARY
or
~~INTELLIGENCE SUMMARY.~~
(Erase heading not required.)

Army Form C. 2118.

Ref Map 36 A N.E.

Place	Date	Hour	Summary of Events and Information	Remarks and references to Appendices
	14th		1 Officer 1 O.R. rank to 15th Corps school for a course in Light Trench Mortars (Lieut HARTERY. M.J. MC) 2 OR from Hospital taken on strength –	
	15th		Battery Training; received orders to "Stand To" and be ready to move at half an hours notice. One gun & team to each Battn (2nd Royal Fusiliers, 1st Lancs Fus, 1st Royal Dublin Fusiliers) 1 Gun and double Team to be held in readiness to move with Brigade Headquarters	
	16th		1 O.R. to 5th Army School for course in Light Trench Mortars. 1 O.R. off strength. "Standing To" Lectures on Stokes Mortars to new men. 3 O.R. Hospital	
	17th		Still "Standing To" Lectures and instruction to untrained men continued.	
	18th		Orders received for 3 guns and teams to report to O.C. 87th T.M. Battery by 6.00 pm on 19.6.18 for special duty in line – Training lectures etc. 29th Divisional "Diamond Troupe" gave a performance in our camp at 6.00 pm. weather fine –	
	19th	11.45	Orders for special duty in line cancelled. 1 O.R. off strength 2 O.Rs Hospital. 1 O.R. Leave to U.K. weather showery.	
	20th		Still "Standing To." Received Brigade Order 236. ref Divisional relief	VI

WS

A7092). Wt. W128 9/M1293 750,000. 1/17. D. D & L., Ltd. Forms/C2118/14.

Instructions regarding War Diaries and Intelligence Summaries are contained in F. S. Regs., Part II. and the Staff Manual respectively. Title pages will be prepared in manuscript.

WAR DIARY
or
~~INTELLIGENCE SUMMARY~~.
(Erase heading not required.)

Army Form C. 2118.

Ref Map 36.A N E

Place	Date	Hour	Summary of Events and Information	Remarks and references to Appendices
	20th		86th Brigade to remain in reserve to 31st Division. Weather showery	
	21st		Training etc	
	22nd		Training etc, weather fine.	
	23rd		Received Brigade order 237 to move on 24th to the BLARINGHAM AREA. 2 O.R. off strength	VII
	24th		Battery moved to BLARINGHEM AREA leaving Camp at C.12.D.5.6 (Ref Map 36A) by march route for PONT D'ASQUIN which was reached by 14.15 and was accomodated in factory at B.8.D.9.7 with Headquarters at B.8.A.6.8. (Ref Map 36A) 1 O.R. off strength. Weather showery.	
	25th		Training etc. weather fine.	
	26th		Received orders from Brigade to send 3 gun teams to the Battns (2nd Royal Fusiliers, 1st Lancs Fus, 1st Royal Dublin Fusiliers) for duty in Reserve line, in support to the 31st and 5th Divisions who were to carry out operations on morning of 28th June. Teams to join Battns at 09 30 27.6.18. Enemy Aeroplanes dropped bombs on our Billet at 00.10 27.6.18. wounding 14. O.R. wounds not serious mostly caused by broken glass. 9. O.R. returned to duty after having their wounds dressed. 1. O.R. off strength	WL

Instructions regarding War Diaries and Intelligence Summaries are contained in F. S. Regs., Part II. and the Staff Manual respectively. Title pages will be prepared in manuscript. (Ref map 36 A NE)

WAR DIARY
or
~~INTELLIGENCE SUMMARY.~~
(Erase heading not required.)

Army Form C. 2118.

Place	Date	Hour	Summary of Events and Information	Remarks and references to Appendices
	27.		2 Gun Teams 1 to 1st Lancs Fusiliers and 1 to 1st Royal Dublin Fusiliers left Brigade Headquarters at 11.30 for duty in line. 1. Gun and Team left with Brigade Headquarters at 16.00 to join the 2nd Royal Fusiliers at D 11. D 4.7 OC at LE TIR ANGLAIS D.17 a 5.4. (Ref map 36 A and 27) Reference Brigade order 229. attached	VIII
	28th		"Standing To" in reserve.	
	29th		Battery "Standing To" until 10.00, when they returned to Battery Hd Qtrs	
	30th		Received Brigade order 241 re move to HEURINGHAM. Lieut HARTERY in advance for Billeting, moved at 14.00 by march route and reached HEURINGHAM at 16.00 and were billeted in Barns at A.14.b.7.4 (Sheet 36 A NW)	IX

L Bowles. Captn
Comdg 86th T.M. Bty

A7092). Wt. W12839/M1293 750,000. 1/17. D. D & L., Ltd. Forms/C2118/14.

~~Copy~~

WRR
DIARY
for
June. 1918

86th
TRENCH MORTAR
BATTERY.
No.........................
Date.........................

86TH
TRENCH MORTAR
BATTERY

No. ....
Date 1. 8. 18

WAR DIARY

For

JULY

1918

LTMB

Army Form C. 2118.

WAR DIARY
or
~~INTELLIGENCE SUMMARY.~~
(Erase heading not required.)

Instructions regarding War Diaries and Intelligence Summaries are contained in F. S. Regs., Part II. and the Staff Manual respectively. Title pages will be prepared in manuscript.

Ref. Map. 36 A NW

Place	Date	Hour	Summary of Events and Information	Remarks and references to Appendices
HEURINGHEM	JULY 1st		Battery cleaning up. weather v. fine.	
	2nd		Training etc. 2 ORs Trench Mortar course XVth Corps School.	
	3rd		Brigade Practice Ceremonial Parade 10.00 hrs.	
	4th	12.00	Ceremonial Parade at A.11.C.0.0. Inspection and presentation of decorations by Genl Sir HERBERT PLUMMER G.C.B. G.C.M.G. G.C.V.O. A.D.C. Comdg 2nd Army. Decorations pinned by Corpl NICHOLLS S.V. MM (2nd Royal Fusiliers) & L.Cpl GAVIN J. MM att 86 T.M. Battery (1st Lancs Fus)	
			Guns were carried on 8 pack mules. weather v. fine. 1 Officer Lieut (E.W. PUTLAND 16th Middx Regt) Leave to U.K. 1 O.R Hospital	
	5th	09.15	Lecture by Col CAMPBELL on Recreational Training at F.11.B.7.0	
			Training etc 1 OR Hospital	
	6th		Training etc.	
	7th		Training etc	
	8th		Training etc firing 60 rounds.	
	9th		Training etc	
	10th		Brigade Sports at A.11.C.0.0. weather showery.	
	11th		Training etc. 16 OR inoculated weather still showery.	
	12th		Training etc	
	13th		Training etc	
	14th		Training etc	
	15th		Training etc 3 OR on strength	[initials]

A7092). Wt. W12839/M1293 750,000. 1/17. D. D & L., Ltd. Forms/C2118/14.

Instructions regarding War Diaries and Intelligence Summaries are contained in F. S. Regs., Part II. and the Staff Manual respectively. Title pages will be prepared in manuscript.

WAR DIARY

or

~~INTELLIGENCE SUMMARY.~~

(Erase heading not required.)

Army Form C. 2118.

Place	Date	Hour	Summary of Events and Information	Remarks and references to Appendices
	July			
HEURINGHEM	16		Received orders to be ready to move to support 31st Division if required	
	17th		Training etc. Order for 31st Division cancelled. Orders received for Divisional Tactical Exercise by 86th Brigade 1. OR Leave to U.K. 2. OR to 2nd Army Rest Camp 2 OR from XV Corp School T. M. course. 3. OR from 2nd Army Rest Camp	
	18th		Divisional Tactical Exercise by 86 Brigade. 3 Guns under Lieut HARTERY	
		09.15	went forward with the 1st R.D.F. starting from F.11.a.6.6. 3 Guns under 2/Lt Smith went forward with the 1st Lancs Fusiliers. (Map Ref Sheets 36 A NE and 36 A NW.) Battery Hd Qtrs with Brigade Hd Qrs at F.11.A.4.4. 12 rounds of ammunition per gun were carried weather fine 1. OR Hospital	
	19th		Training etc.	
	20th		Brigade Tactical Exercise. 3 Trench Mortars under ~~2/Lt Smith~~ Lieut HARTERY	
		09.15	went forward with 1st R.D.F. starting from F.11.c.7.8. 12 shells per gun were carried. Remainder of Battery training. 1 OR Hospital	
	21st	22.30	Received orders from Brigade re move on 22nd	
NOORDPEENE	22nd	07.45	Battery moved by march route to NOORDPEENE (Ref map sheet 27) and were accomodated in a Barn at N.5.b.3.6. NOORDPEENE was reached at 14.20. 1 Officer (Lieut HARTERY) and 1. OR advance party, weather fine and hot. 3. OR fell out on march 1 OR off strength	
	23rd		Training etc weather v. wet	
	24th		Training etc	
	25		Training. 2 Officers to reconnoitre two positions "A" & "B" routes (order att.)	WB

A7092). Wt. W12839/M1293 750,000. 1/17. D. D & L., Ltd. Forms/C2118/14.

Instructions regarding War Diaries and Intelligence Summaries are contained in F. S. Regs., Part II. and the Staff Manual respectively. Title pages will be prepared in manuscript.

WAR DIARY
or
~~INTELLIGENCE SUMMARY.~~
(Erase heading not required.)

Army Form C. 2118.

Place	Date	Hour	Summary of Events and Information	Remarks and references to Appendices
NOORDPEENE	26th		Training etc. 1. Officer to reconnoitre A & B routes.	
	27th		Training etc.	
	28th		Training etc 1. OR Hospital - 1 OR leave to U.K.	
	29th		Training Route March	
	30th		Training - 4. OR from each Battn (2nd Royal Fusiliers, 1st Lancs Fus) and 1st Royal Dublin Fusiliers) came under instructions from 86th Brigade for a course of instruction in Trench Mortars	
	31st		Training etc Received Brigade Operation order no 241. 1 OR from Hospital - weather v. fine and hot.	

W. Bowes
Captn
Comdg 86th T.M. Bty

A7092). Wt. W12839/M1293. 750,000. 1/17. D. D & L., Ltd. Forms/C2118/14.

86th Trench Mortar Battery

War Diary

for

August. 1918

86TH
TRENCH MORTAR
BATTERY.

No.........
Date 1.9.18

WAR DIARY

FOR

AUGUST 1918

Instructions regarding War Diaries and Intelligence Summaries are contained in F. S. Regs., Part II. and the Staff Manual respectively. Title pages will be prepared in manuscript.

WAR DIARY
or
INTELLIGENCE SUMMARY.
(Erase heading not required.)

Army Form C. 2118.

Place	Date	Hour	Summary of Events and Information	Remarks and references to Appendices
NOORDPEENE	1-8-18		The Battery moved with 86th Infantry Bde by march route to V.22 c 3.2 (Sheet 27). Starting point was passed at scheduled time and destination was reached at 23-10 hrs. Battery was accommodated in 1 Tent and 7 Shelters. During the latter part of march Hostile aircraft dropped several bombs on road between HONDEGHEM and HAZEBROUCK. Casualties nil. 1 O.R from Leave. Weather fine. B Order No 241 attached.	I
	2-8-18		Battery proceeded to BORRE at 21-00 hrs. Accommodated in billets at W.19.a.1.2 and W.19.a.2.1. The latter being Battery H.Qs. (Sheet 27) Weather Wet.	
BORRE	3-8-18		Battery Training. Gun Drill etc. Bde Order No 242 attached	II
"	4-8-18		Eight guns & teams proceeded to line to take over from 121st T.M.B. Four guns were taken to front line and four in support line. FWD Battery H.Q. at STRAZEELE STN LIEUT E RUTLAND i/c. Battery H.Q. remained at W.19.a.2.1 (Sheet 27) Weather wet. 2 O.R. from Rest Camp. Casualties nil.	

CWB

(A9475) Wt W2358/P360 600,000 12/17 D. D. & L. Sch. 52a. Forms/C2118/15

Instructions regarding War Diaries and Intelligence Summaries are contained in F. S. Regs., Part II. and the Staff Manual respectively. Title pages will be prepared in manuscript.

WAR DIARY
or
INTELLIGENCE SUMMARY.
(*Erase heading not required.*)

Army Form C. 2118.

Place	Date	Hour	Summary of Events and Information	Remarks and references to Appendices
BORRE	5-8-18		Two front line guns were withdrawn to Rear Battery H.Q. also two from Support line. The latter were laid to cover STRAZEELE STATION. The two guns in front line were pushed forward to CYPRUS FARM (E.12.c.4.9) (Sheet 36A NE. 7A)	
	6-8-18		On the night of 6-8-18 at the request of Infantry in line 120 rounds were fired on to E.M.G. emplacement in CELERY COPSE. Good results were obtained. Weather wet. Visibility Poor owing to haze. Casualties Nil.	
	7-8-18		Battery in line. No firing done. Teams in line and reserve engaged in salvage work. Weather fine. Casualties Nil.	
	8-8-18		Teams in line engaged in bringing ammunition forward from old front line positions. 20 Shells ready prepared in sandbags ready to go forward with infantry patrols. 20 Mules brought up supply of shells to forward position.	
	9-8-18		Teams in line. 100 rounds were fired on CYNDE FARM and CELERY COPSE at request of infantry to engage E.M.G.	[illegible signature]

Instructions regarding War Diaries and Intelligence Summaries are contained in F. S. Regs., Part II, and the Staff Manual respectively. Title pages will be prepared in manuscript.

WAR DIARY
or
INTELLIGENCE SUMMARY.
(Erase heading not required.)

Army Form C. 2118.

Place	Date	Hour	Summary of Events and Information	Remarks and references to Appendices
DOGRE	10-8-18		Teams in line were relieved by Support Teams. LIEUT HAGTERY relieved LIEUT RUTLAND	
"	11-8-18		Two guns in line assisted the 1st LAN FUS in their attempt to advance the line. At request of infantry one gun was placed in position to fire on E. post at LYNDE FARM. Gun was to fire until white light was sent up by O.C. Coy. This was done after 50 rounds had been fired. Post was then rushed by patrol and two prisoners captured. Later on in night 30 rounds were fired on ditch running N. from F.13.b.6.8. Weather fine. Visibility good. Casualties nil. 214 Bde Order attached	III
	12-8-18		Teams in line. Fired 25 rounds on line of railway track E. of CELERY COPSE in co-operation with Artillery. In the evening enemy put down heavy barrage with shells of all calibres, under which he counter-attacked. The gun team in line fired 80 rounds to cover [illegible]	WB

Instructions regarding War Diaries and Intelligence Summaries are contained in F. S. Regs., Part II. and the Staff Manual respectively. Title pages will be prepared in manuscript.

WAR DIARY
or
INTELLIGENCE SUMMARY.
(Erase heading not required.)

Army Form C. 2118.

Place	Date	Hour	Summary of Events and Information	Remarks and references to Appendices
BORRE	12.5.18		of our infantry. The guns were then dismounted and were withdrawn to old position at CYPRUS FARM. During day 1 O.R. was killed and 3 O.R. wounded by bomb dropped by E. low flying aeroplane. Weather fair.	
"	13.5.18		50 Rounds were fired on LYNDE FARM and vicinity.	
"	14.5.18		Battery relief for teams in front line. 2/Lt SMITH relieves Lieut HARTERY. 2 guns in front line 2 guns in Support.	
"	15.5.18		Teams in line engaged line of railway trenches E of CRUCK COPSE in conjunction with artillery. Later in the day LYNDE FARM was engaged. 40 rounds being expended.	
	16.5.18		Received Bde order No 247. 6 guns were placed in line to take part in operation by 9th and 29th Divisions. The object to improve our positions along the HOEGENACKER RIDGE and to kill germans. Positions for guns selected and prepared. Addendum to Bde Order 247 received.	IV. V
			Amendment No 1 and No 2 to Bde Order No 247 received.	VI VII

(A9175) Wt W2358/P360 600,000 12/17 D. D. & L. Sch. 52a. Forms/C2118/15

WB

Instructions regarding War Diaries and Intelligence Summaries are contained in F. S. Regs., Part II. and the Staff Manual respectively. Title pages will be prepared in manuscript.

WAR DIARY
or
INTELLIGENCE SUMMARY.
(Erase heading not required.)

Army Form C. 2118.

Place	Date	Hour	Summary of Events and Information	Remarks and references to Appendices
BERRÉ	18.7.18		Amendment No 3 to Bde Order received. Zero hour fixed for 11 AM. T.M. targets to be line of trench E. of CELERY COPSE. Firing commenced zero + 1 to zero + 15 with 4 guns at same time 2 guns fired on LYNDE FARM. Smoke and H.E. shells were used. At zero + 40 to zero + 50. 2 guns fired on LYNDE FARM with common shell. From zero + 90 to zero 110. 4 guns again fired on trench, also 2 guns on LYNDE FARM. Owing to great enemy defence of railway trench the enemy was not driven out and our attacking troops were forced to withdraw. 520 rounds were expended during this operation.	VIII
			Bde Order No 248 received.	IX
	19.7.18		Amendment to Bde Order No 248 received. Preparation made for attack by 86th Bde to capture the line E.13 central to junction of METEREN BECQUE and railway line E.2.c. Zero hour 5.0 pm. 6 mortars in position at 2 pm. Targets line of railway trench S of E.7.c.6.4. The mortars	

WB

Instructions regarding War Diaries and Intelligence Summaries are contained in F. S. Regs., Part II, and the Staff Manual respectively. Title pages will be prepared in manuscript.

WAR DIARY
or
INTELLIGENCE SUMMARY.
(*Erase heading not required.*)

Army Form C. 2118.

Place	Date	Hour	Summary of Events and Information	Remarks and references to Appendices
BORRE	19-5-18		were to fire from zero to zero + 3. 150 rounds were thus expended. Four Mortars were then pushed forward to vicinity of LYNDE FARM and LESAGE FARM with a good supply of shells to cover targets at F.12.b.2.0. and F.11.a.4.9. 2 O.R. were killed and 3 O.R. wounded during this operation. 20 Mules were utilized for carrying ammunition forward.	Artillery Order No 55
"	20-5-18		After the operation of 19-5-18 the mortars were in position selected and on the 20th four guns & teams were withdrawn from the line to Rear Battery H.Qs at BORRE leaving 2 guns in position at LESAGE FARM covering S.O.S line.	
	21-5-18		Teams in line relieved. Lieut PUTLAND took over from 2/Lt SMITH.	
"	22-5-18		The two mortars at LESAGE FARM were withdrawn. All the teams were engaged on salvage work. Good results were obtained. Shells from various emplacements were collected and placed in central position.	
	23-5-18		Teams in line on salvage work. Remainder of Battery doing	[initials]

Army Form C. 2118.

WAR DIARY
or
INTELLIGENCE SUMMARY.
(Erase heading not required.)

Instructions regarding War Diaries and Intelligence Summaries are contained in F. S. Regs., Part II, and the Staff Manual respectively. Title pages will be prepared in manuscript.

Place	Date	Hour	Summary of Events and Information	Remarks and references to Appendices
[illegible]	23.8.18		Training etc at R. Battery H.Q. Two officers of the Battery reconnoitred dug-outs at F.9.c.5.2 to F.9.d.4.3. While doing so stick bombs were thrown at them followed by rifle and M.G. fire from enemy post at F.9.d.5.7. Papers and documents brought back by the patrol identified several field artillery batteries in this sector.	
"	24.8.18		Battery relief. Lt HARTERY relieved Lt PURLAND. Gun teams on salvage work.	
"	25.8.18		Gun teams at FWD H.Qs on salvage work. Remainder training at R.H.Qs. Pte Jacques awarded Military Medal.	
"	26.8.18		Teams on salvage work. Results very good.	
"	27.8.18		" " " " " " "	
"	28.8.18		" " " " " " "	
"	29.8.18		Gun team in line relieved. Relieving party engaged in Salvage work.	
"	30.8.18		Lt PURLAND relieved Lt HARTERY at Fwd Battery H.Q. Teams went to KISMET HOUSE but later on were ordered to return to STRAZEELE STN.	
"	31.8.18		Battery moved from FWD. H.Qs and Rear H.Q. to W.28.a.7.3 where the men were accommodated in dug-outs near W.28.a.7.3 with Battery H.Q. in W.28.a.7.3.	

(A9175) Wt W2358/P560 600,000 12/17 D. D. & L. Sch. 52a. Forms/C2118/15

1200 Rounds were fired during the month.

W Bowles Capt
Cmdg 86th T.M. Bty

www.ingramcontent.com/pod-product-compliance
Lightning Source LLC
Chambersburg PA
CBHW081408160426
43193CB00013B/2134